BRITISH AIRBORNE TROOPS

BRITISH AIRBORNE TROOPS 1940-45
Barry Gregory

DOUBLEDAY & COMPANY, INC.
Garden City, New York

Contents

Printed in Great Britain

Copyright © 1974 Barry Gregory
First published in Great Britain in 1974 by
Macdonald and Jane's, London

ISBN 0-385-04247-7

Library of Congress Catalog Card Number 74-9157

Layout and make-up: Michael Jarvis

Maps: Peter Sarson and Tony Bryan

Major-General 'Boy' Browning and Winston Churchill in 1943.

Introduction

After the fall of France in June 1940, the British people stood alone, protected only by the Royal Navy; the moat of the Channel, an army almost devoid of guns, and fifty-nine fighter squadrons of the Royal Air Force. Winston Churchill's apparent motive at that time in suggesting the immediate formation of 'a corps of at least 5,000 parachute troops' had the true Churchillian style but many Service planners were less enthusiastic about the project. Military policy which conceived of taking the war on land to the enemy had the appearance of a welcome but impractical gesture of defiance. Churchill, however, had then held the reins of supreme command for only a month but he had already jolted the national mood for passive resistance with more than one defiant gesture. His memoranda to the Joint Chiefs of Staff had indeed discussed several new military concepts more clearly grasped in a context of the offensive.

In April and May the Germans had convincingly demonstrated the effectiveness of parachute, air-transported and gliderborne troops in Norway, Denmark and the Low Countries. The conquest of Holland by *Generaloberst* Kurt Student's *Luftlandekorps* did more prior to the Battle of Britain to convince the British nation of the threat of invasion than did the military disaster in France. But in spite of the parachute scare that undoubtedly prevailed in Britain throughout the summer of 1940, it is doubtful if even the Prime Minister had made more than a cursory evaluation of the true potential of airborne forces. Churchill was more likely to have been of the opinion that if German troops could jump out of aeroplanes then the British Army should learn to do so as well!

The Central Landing School was thus formed at RAF Ringway near Manchester and RAF and Army staffs were recruited to organise parachute training and evolve the logistics of airborne assault. The many thousands of British soldiers who have learned to parachute safely since those early days at Ringway must all feel a special sense of gratitude for the courage and resourcefulness of the pioneer jumping instructors as well as of the pupils who participated in their experiments. Many a cliché has been coined in Army language about the noble art of parachuting. 'Dicing with death' is perhaps the most familiar expression that comes to mind. The motto of No. 1 Parachute Training School – 'Knowledge dispels fear' – commends itself, however, to more serious attention. This axiom provides a powerful incentive to the intelligent student of dangerous pursuits and in the case of parachuting loses nothing in integrity for not being absolutely true.

If at first a parachute battalion was thought to be a bit of a stunt the circus days were over after the *Luftlandekorps* invasion of Crete in May 1941. Before the battle was over Winston Churchill spoke again about airborne matters. ' . . . We ought to have an Airborne Division on the German model, with any improvements which might suggest themselves from experience.' Thereafter events moved more swiftly in the development of British airborne forces.

The scope of this short, illustrated book is intended to trace the development of the airborne method in Britain and to relate the training and battle narratives of 1st and 6th Airborne Divisions. Illustrated books of this kind tend to be written to a rigid publisher's brief that specifies the number of words and illustrations that the author is allowed to supply. With so much exciting material at my disposal the problem has inevitably been to know how best to award the priorities and to satisfy my conscience that the omissions are justified.

An airborne division comprised many elements: the Parachute Regiment, the glider pilots and gliderborne infantry and the essential support and service units. My aim has been to describe how an airborne division worked and what 1st and 6th Airborne achieved during the Second World War. I believe that in the past many of the authors who have written so well about British airborne forces have neglected the work of the Parachute Training School and the tremendous influence that the exemplary standards set by the jumping instructors continued to exert on parachute troops throughout their careers. I think, too, that the rôle of the Glider Pilot Regiment and the exploits of the six County battalions that flew in the gliders has been overlooked. I hope that in the following pages I have struck a proper balance between the training background and the respective contributions of all airborne units in training and in battle.

The relegation of the Special Air Service Regiment, General Wingate's Second Chindit Operations and 44th Indian Airborne Division to the appendices is by no means intended as an assessment of their importance. The SAS properly belongs to the theme of British airborne troops but the Regiment's links with the airborne divisions were tenuous. Although early in 1944 the SAS Brigade was placed under the command of General Browning's Airborne Corps, the arrangement was largely a matter of administrative convenience. The SAS story is a worthy subject for study in its own right. The Chindits paradoxically had no connection with the airborne divisions and should really be assessed in the context of the war in Burma. The development of 44th Indian Airborne Division was overtaken by events. If the war had gone on longer, this fine division would certainly have had an important job to do in the Far East.

Above all, I hope that the book conveys the essential spirit and good humour of British Airborne Troops.

Acknowledgements

I should like to thank Brian L. Davis for advice on uniform detail and help with collecting airborne insignia. I am also grateful to Marion Andrews for typing the manuscript.

The information given in Appendix 3 is based on the relevant sections of the official *Orders of Battle* of the British Army compiled for the Cabinet Office, Historical Section, by H. F. Joslen and published in 1960 by Her Majesty's Stationery Office.

Unless otherwise stated the photographs in this book are Crown Copyright and reproduced by kind permission of the Imperial War Museum.

Finally I must thank my many friends from parachuting days whose example in times past has been the source of my inspiration in recent months. *Ad unum omnes.*

BARRY GREGORY

1. Parachute Commando

On 10th May 1940 after a belated revolt in government circles Winston Churchill was popularly acclaimed as Britain's Prime Minister. In the early hours of that day two German Army Groups had launched full-scale offensives into the Low Countries and France. Within hours von Bock's Army Group B had secured vital objectives in Belgium and Holland. Further south von Rundstedt's Army Group A stationed between the Meuse and the Moselle successfully exploited a weak link in the Allied defensive system in the difficult terrain of the Ardennes forest. A screen of Belgian troops was brushed aside and the German Panzer columns moved swiftly into France. Before nightfall the fate of Britain's Continental allies had been sealed and the withdrawal of the British Army from France was imminent.

Early days at RAF Ringway. Britain's first paratroopers on parade with their despatchers. Each section or stick of ten men represents one planeload. The original Whitley carrier aircraft can be seen in the background.

Few supremos in history can have been faced with such daunting prospects on their first day in office. When Holland surrendered on 14th May, three-quarters of Germany's total armoured strength was driving across France to the English Channel. Allied participation in the month-old Norwegian campaign was now doomed and British and French forces were evacuated during 4th–8th June. On 27th May and prior to the Belgian capitulation the British Expeditionary Force in France fell back on a shallow perimeter based on canal and river lines near Dunkirk.

During the next seven days 233,039 British troops as well as 112,546 Allied troops were lifted from the beaches of Dunkirk by British, Dutch, Belgian and French ships. Dunkirk was indeed a great deliverance for Britain but Churchill was prompt to remind the nation that wars are not won by evacuations; certainly not by evacuations in which the army leaves its guns, its tanks and its vehicles behind.

On 6th June the Prime Minister sent a challenging memorandum to General Lord Ismay, whose military function it was to convey the instructions of the War Cabinet to the Joint Chiefs of Staff. Churchill wrote: 'The passive resistance war, in which we have acquitted ourselves so well, must come to an end. I look to the Joint Chiefs of Staff to propose me measures for a vigorous, enterprising and ceaseless offensive against the whole German occupied coastline.'

The French Armistice was not concluded until 22nd June but the Prime Minister already had visions of launching 'butcher and bolt' raids on enemy-held territory. His memorandum included demands for the development of tank landing craft, intelligence and espionage systems, 'striking companies' and 'parachute troops on a scale equal to five thousand'. Churchill's instructions were received by the Service planners with scepticism. The idea of taking the war to the enemy on land in Europe was thought to be impractical and the formation of parachute units moreover logistically unsound. The Prime Minister's memorandum could not be ignored, however, and action followed in many directions.

The tank landing craft and amphibious vessels that emerged from the drawing boards as a result of Churchill's directive are the subject of another story. The various needs for information from within the Axis homelands and occupied territories were answered by the establishment of the Special Operations Executive (SOE). This clandestine military organisation was to spread its network of intelligence and subversion throughout Europe, the Mediterranean theatre and South East Asia. What of the 'striking companies' and parachute troops?

Lieutenant-Colonel Dudley Clarke had already thought of an idea for raising irregular units to strike at an enemy whose forces now stretched out from Narvik to the Pyrenees. Clarke was Military Assistant to the Chief of the Imperial General Staff, General Sir John Dill. On 5th June Clarke told Dill about his plan. On the following day Dill told the Prime Minister, who was obviously apprised of Clarke's ideas when on the same day he wrote to Ismay. Two days later Dudley Clarke was ordered to mount a raid across the Channel at the earliest possible opportunity.

Winston Churchill's enthusiasm for Clarke's *modus operandi* induced the former to suggest to the C-in-C Home Forces that 10,000 men should immediately be drawn from existing units to form 'Storm Troop' or

'Leopard' battalions. The officers and men should be lightly armed with automatic weapons and grenades and supplied with motor-cycles and armoured cars. In addition to their rôle as special raiding forces the men were to be ready for lightning action on the home beaches in the event of an invasion.

The 'striking companies' or Commandos as they were soon called met with less resistance from the Service planners than had at first been anticipated. The Army's principal aim of course in 1940 was to train infantry soldiers and tank crews; few battalion commanders enjoyed losing their best men to the new Commandos. But viewed in cold perspective at a more senior level, the volunteer costs the Army no more to acquire than the reluctant conscript and the rigorous training of self-sufficient Commando units was no great strain on available resources. Ten Commando groups with an original establishment of 500 men each were accordingly raised from the Regular Army and Royal Marines.

On 22nd June the Prime Minister brought up the business of parachute troops again with the Joint Chiefs of Staff in a communication tabbed ACTION THIS DAY. 'We ought to have a corps of at least 5,000 parachute troops . . . I hear that something is being done already to form such a corps but only, I believe, on a very small scale. Advantage must be taken of the summer to train these forces, who can none the less play their part meanwhile as shock troops in home defence.'

The chief resistance to the 'parachute' commando idea came understandably from the Royal Air Force. Earlier in the month a conference urgently convened at the Air Ministry had agreed to establish a parachute training centre. But the RAF simply could not spare enough aircraft to mount an effective airborne operation. Manchester Corporation's civil airport at Ringway was chosen as the home of the new unit. RAF Ringway was to be a combined services establishment with the title of 'The Central Landing School', and the RAF and Army were to work together on the staff.

No. 2 Commando was assigned to Ringway for parachute training along with six obsolete Whitley bombers. Pilot Officer Louis Strange DSO, MC, DFC, a former 1914–18 fighter ace and sometime Lieutenant-Colonel in the Army, was to be in charge of parachuting at the new school. The RAF's battle commitment, however, was not scheduled to exceed the supply of enough converted Whitleys to drop a total of 720 fully-armed men and 62,000 lbs of equipment.

On 9th April the remarkable German seaborne invasion of Norway was accelerated by the seizure of Oslo and Stavanger by Luftwaffe paratroopers and airborne infantry. The swift occupation of Oslo was made possible by the air-landing in Junkers transport planes of the 1st and 2nd Companies drawn from 1st Bn *Fallschirmjäger-Regiment 1* followed into Fornebu airport by the 324th Infantry Regiment. The 3rd Company from the same battalion of FJR 1 made a successful drop at Stavanger and was assisted in the capture of the town by air-transported troops from the 193rd Infantry Regiment.

Meanwhile in Denmark in the early hours of the same day the 4th Company (1st Bn FJR 1) was dropped at Aalborg on Jutland and at both ends of the 3,500 metre-long Vordingborg bridge that connects the islands of Falster and Zeeland. The capture of the bridge enabled motorised infantry disembarking at the ferry-port of Gedser to advance immediately on Copenhagen.

The landing of German troops by air into battle did not entirely take the Allies by surprise. The existence since 1936 of the parachute training school at Stendal was well known. In September 1939 *Generaloberst* Kurt Student's airborne corps comprised *Fliegerdivision 7* as a parachute force and the 22nd Division as a predominantly air-landed force. The corps was equipped with a formidable fleet of obsolete Ju 52 bombers converted to the transport rôle and fifty DFS-230 gliders.

On 10th May Student's *Luftlandekorps* struck in strength as the spearhead of von Bock's Army Group B advancing into Belgium and Holland. Before first light, Assault Group Koch took to the air above Cologne in Ju 52s alongside *Oberleutnant* Witzig's party of gliderborne parachute engineers. The destination of the *Fallschirmjäger* was the Belgian fortress of Eban-Emael and nearby bridges on the Albert Canal between Maastricht and Liège. Whilst *Hauptmann* Koch's parachutists attacked the bridges at Veldwezelt, Vroenhoven and Canne, seven of the eleven DFS-230 gliders that had slipped their tow ropes before crossing the Dutch panhandle north-west of Aachen landed on top of the sleeping fortress. Witzig's party of fifty-five engineers succeeded in destroying two 120-mm cannons and nine 75-mm guns. When the exits of the fortress were blown in or covered by the fire of the engineers the 700-strong Belgian garrison was trapped. Next morning, 11th May, the *Fallschirmjäger* were relieved and the area was secured for the advance of the main ground forces.

The invasion of Holland was preceded by heavy air raids on The Hague, Rotterdam and further south as far as the south bank of the Maas estuary. In the early morning 475 Ju 52s crossed the Dutch frontier covered by a thick fighter screen. In the north in the area of The Hague a battalion of paratroopers and six infantry battalions from the 22nd Division were dropped and air-landed at locations at Valkenburg, Ypenburg and Ockenburg. A further parachute drop was made at Delft. In the south four battalions from FJR 1 and FJR 2 of *Fliegerdivision 7* were deployed at Rotterdam (Waalhaven), Dordrecht and Moerdijk. As the parachutists seized the Maas crossing after their descents at Dordrecht and Moerdijk, a heavy contingent of infantry supported by *Fallschirmjäger* were flown into the Waalhaven airport on the outskirts of Rotterdam. The brief campaign in Holland was over four days later.

In July a separate British Combined Operations Command under the Joint Chiefs of Staff was formed to study and implement Commando warfare. Admiral of the Fleet Sir Roger Keyes of Zeebrugge fame was shortly appointed Director of Combined Operations. The development of parachuting techniques and an operational airborne unit was to be the responsibility of the Central Landing School. The RAF was to be responsible for the air side of the development and training, the Army for the military subjects. The operational employment of the trained cadre was to be initiated by the War Office, but the actual planning and carrying out of such operations devolved upon the Director of Combined Operations.

A German paratrooper's helmet and odd items of equipment conveyed from Rotterdam were studied with interest by senior officers.

Group Captain L. G. Harvey was in command at Ringway where the organisation was renamed the Central Landing Establishment and expanded by the inclusion of a glider section. Major John Rock of the Royal Engineers was the senior Army staff officer in charge of Army development and Wing Commander Sir Nigel Norman was his opposite number on the Air side. Louis Strange, soon a squadron leader, was responsible for the actual training of the parachutists.

The German paratrooper presented an awesome example to airborne planners in Britain as well as to the C-in-C Home Forces. Thousands of square miles of the United Kingdom were covered with obstacles to prevent the landing of transport planes and gliders and with a view to impaling parachutists. Such intelligence as was received in Britain after the devastating events of April and May was unfortunately so false and distorted by rumour and propaganda as to be meaningless.

The *Fallschirmjäger*, who wore a steel helmet, a long, grey, green, brown and black combat smock, baggy trousers and special jump boots, usually carried a 9-mm Schmeisser sub-machine-gun (MP 38). Student's burly harlequins were aggressive but well disciplined and fought in a strictly military manner. A booklet circulating in Britain as late as 1941 stated nevertheless that the German 'Parachute Corps' leapt into action disguised *inter alios* as parsons, butchers' boys and nuns. The Home Guard (LDV) – raised in May 1940 as a result of the parachute scare – were advised that the sky invaders were fitted out with boots with spring devices. Marksmen were informed that the parachutist was at his most vulnerable when caught 'on the bounce' on first making contact with the ground.

The idea of airborne forces was by no means new. In the First World War the difficulty of swiftly communicating indirect target references to the guns led to the introduction of the Army observation balloon. The captive balloon was controlled by windlass and cable from a mobile truck. Supported by 37,500 cubic feet of hydrogen contained in a gas bag made of rubberised cloth, two officers slung in the look-out basket could, on a fine day, comfortably observe activity on the ground from an altitude of up to 5,000 feet over a radius of ten miles or more.

The operational life of the captive balloon used widely by the opposing armies was reckoned to be fifteen days; and German airmen rated balloon-busting as being worth $1\frac{1}{2}$ planes per balloon for the record. But for the parachute, casualties among balloon spotters would have been enormous. The British airborne gunners used the 'Guardian Angel' type or the attached-type Spencer 'chute packed into a container hung on the side of the basket. The Spencer harness was not adjustable and many of the men made their own from rope. When a balloon was set on fire the time margin for escape was negligible. No small amount of nerve was necessary, however, to make the effort and escapees were often unmercifully strafed in mid-air by the attacking plane.

In March 1916 a lone aircraft of the Royal Naval Air Service took off in Mesopotamia in response to a request from Major-General Townshend and flew to the besieged British garrison at Kut-al-Amara. There the naval pilot dropped a millstone weighing 70 lbs. This was the first time in the history of British Service flying that an attempt was made to supply ground forces by air. During the following month a RNAS detachment

Over the Western Front in 1916. Two artillery spotters ascending in baskets suspended from a Caquot balloon. Note the parachute bags slung over the sides of the baskets. The average operational life of an observer balloon was fifteen days.

dropped over seven tons of food, and mail, wireless batteries and medical equipment before the ill-fated garrison surrendered to the Turkish Army. By the beginning of 1917 supply by air was commonly practised in Europe and in November of that year large quantities of ammunition were dropped to Allied troops during the Battle of Vittorio Veneto in Italy.

Secret missions were carried out with success by parachutists on the Western Front, in Italy, in Austria and in Russia. Winston Churchill advocated dropping fighting columns to destroy bridges: a small French parachute group jumped in the Ardennes in 1918; but the only significant contribution to the development of airborne battle tactics at this time was made by a one-star American general known throughout the Service as Billy Mitchell. This young American, who had played a leading part in the organisation of the Air Service of the American Expeditionary Force, thought up a daring plan for dropping the United States 1st Division from British Handley-Page bombers to capture the fortress city of Metz.

As it happened when the Victory offensive was launched in September 1918, Metz was no longer located on the American line of advance but the American C-in-C, General Pershing, had already shelved the plan actually prepared by Lieutenant-Colonel Lewis Brereton 'until 1919'. After the war Billy Mitchell, as assistant chief of the United States Air Service, pleaded the case for strength through air power and his theory of 'vertical envelop-

1918. A
'Guardian Angel'
parachute. The test
parachutist is a
woman.

ment' by parachute troops. His critical attitudes in matters of defence resulted, however, in his suspension from the Service in 1925. His reputation was vindicated by the turn of world events after his death in 1936 and the posthumous reinstatement of his general's rank.

In 1922 the Royal Air Force accepted the twin-engined Vickers Vernon as a troop carrier and the following year Nos 45 and 70 Squadrons flew troops into action against insurgents in Irak. Ten years later when trouble brewed again in the same country twenty-one Vickers Victoria troop carriers transported the 1st Northamptons into battle in two lifts. The Italian Regia Aeronautica, which between the World Wars was one of the most advanced air forces in the world, dropped paratroopers at Cinsello near Milan in November 1927. The Italians used the Salvator 'chute, which was operated by hand grip on the belt or static-line, but the primary focus in Italy was on air-landing techniques.

During the 1930s the Russians vigorously applied themselves to airborne training as well as to parachuting for fun. Commissar for Defence Comrade Voroshiloff was generous in his praise of the Russian parachutist and it was said that over a million men and women belonged to civilian clubs.

In September 1936 in the Minsk area the future Field-Marshal Earl Wavell witnessed a demonstration drop by 1,500 infantry soldiers.

Soviet Army manoeuvres in the 1930s revealed that Marshal Tuchachevski's airborne forces were well advanced in military parachute and air-landing techniques. This shot from a newsreel shows Russian paratroopers climbing through a hatch in the roof of an Antonov bomber and descending by free fall. The height is about 2,000 feet.

During the same exercise a mechanised formation including trucks, three-ton tanks, light armoured cars and light guns were hung between the wheels of Antonov bombers and dropped by parachute. Wavell was much intrigued at his first sight of this novel method of making war. At this time too the Red Army was already experimenting in the use of gliders towed both singly and in tandem. In 1941 the Red Army boasted three airborne corps and three specialist brigades.

The Russian airborne manoeuvres of 1935 and 1936 caused no eyebrows to be raised by the senior members of the military hierarchies of Britain and the United States. The Americans like the British had given some study to the air transport or air-landing concept but little or none to parachute and glider training. In the 1920s the United States Marine Corps experimented with aviation for evacuating the sick and wounded on minor expeditionary duties. Then in 1932 Captain George C. Kenney surprised all concerned on an exercise in Delaware when he flew in an infantry section on a tactical mission. Small-scale experiments in parachuting men and weapons were also conducted at Kelly and Brook Fields, Texas.

Britain's attitude might best be summed up by the official reaction to General Wavell's report on the 1936 manoeuvres in the Soviet Union. Unlike his German companion on the trip – Kurt Student – Wavell's considered opinion was that paratroopers would not materially affect the trend of military operations. The Secretary of State for War had already viewed a Russian training film at the War Office featuring 2,000 airborne troops dropped to capture an airfield. But this kind of soldier was expensive to train, equip and maintain and money was hard enough to come by even for home defence in 1936.

The RAF first adopted the parachute for pilots as a life-saving aid in 1918. In 1925 the Irvin 28-ft 'A' type replaced the original 'Guardian Angel' 'chute for official use. Leslie Irvin, the American parachute pioneer and stuntman, emigrated to Britain a year later and set up his factory at Letchworth in Hertfordshire, where it flourishes to this day. Later the 24-ft emergency 'chute was accepted for pilots but the 28-ft version remained in service for training purposes. A parachute training unit was formed at Henlow, Bedfordshire, and airmen were taught to pack their own parachutes and jump from a Vickers Vimy biplane flying at 500 feet. A special platform was erected on one of the bracing struts between the wings. The learner mounted the platform and, after pulling his rip cord, he was pulled away as the wind filled his parachute canopy.

New personalities began to influence the parachute world in the early 1930s. Raymond Quilter, a former Guards officer and a keen amateur pilot, met James Gregory, an experienced worker in the parachute field. Gregory and his wife had already made an experimental emergency 'chute, cheap enough for private fliers to buy. In 1934 the Gregory-Quilter team set up the GQ Company to make parachutes for the RAF, private fliers and civil airlines. The civil airlines rejected the idea of issuing parachutes to their passengers but when the storm clouds gathered over Munich and war seemed inevitable, the GQ Company was at last seriously in business. Their new factory at Woking, Surrey, was designed to make 24-ft emergency 'chutes, but Quilter and Gregory also worked on a larger version, 28 feet in diameter and with a static-line, for parachute troops.

On 9th July 1940 before any descents had been made at Ringway, the first pupil parachutists commenced a course of ground training. They were men of 'B' and 'C' Troops of No 2 Commando. Louis Strange turned to RAF Henlow and appropriated their supply of 28-ft Irvin training parachutes along with the services of Flight-Sergeant 'Bill' Brereton and eight fabric workers willing to act as parachute jumping instructors. About this time a party of NCOs from the Army Physical Training Corps similarly volunteered as instructors and reported at Ringway.

The first live descent was made from a Whitley on 13th July at the nearby Tatton Park by the 'pull-off' method. The door of the Whitley bomber was too small for the men to jump from so an open cockpit was improvised for exits by removing the rear gun turret. There was just room for a pupil facing forwards to stand up in the cockpit holding on to a steel bar. The rip cord was operated by a line attached to a strongpoint on the aircraft. In the earliest days only one man jumped at a time as the Whitley flew across the dropping zone at 100 mph, but it was realised that on operations the men must jump in rapid succession. A circular hole or 'aperture' as it was officially known was accordingly made in the floor of the fuselage. The men in the aircraft crawled on hands and knees to the exit position through the dark interior of the fuselage, which was cramped, draughty and inclined to be odorous.

Above

When the Whitleys were first converted for parachuting the rear gun turret was removed to provide an exit platform.. This method of jumping was laborious but the introduction of the hole in the floor of the fuselage enabled ten men to jump in quick succession.

Above right

Interior of a Whitley in flight. The third man on the left is sitting beside the hole.

More descents were made, some from the platform and some through the floor. The parachutists in the Whitley were carried five forward and five aft of the exit hole; the jumping sequence alternating between forward and aft. After hooking their lines to the strongpoint the men in turn swung their feet into the hole in the sitting position. On the green light signal and the despatcher's peremptory command to 'GO', the parachutist dropped through the hole with his arms to the side and body erect. The hole, which was thirty inches across by nearly three feet deep, tapered slightly like a funnel at the bottom. As the lower end of the body entered the slip stream the tendency was for the legs to be lifted resulting for many in a violent smack in the face. Few parachutists survived the course without 'ringing the bell' or suffering the 'Whitley kiss' as the hazard was otherwise known. A well-trained stick of ten men made its departure through the hole in nine or ten seconds.

All seemed to go well until 25th July when after 135 jumps at the school a pupil's parachute failed to develop properly. Driver Evans fell straight to the ground and was instantly killed. His death caused a stoppage of live parachuting while an investigation was made into the cause of the accident. Dummies were fitted out with parachutes and dropped during a demonstration but three more failures were incurred. The fault appeared to lie in the adapting of the Irvin trainer parachute for automatic pulling of the rip cord. With this type the canopy was withdrawn from the bag before the rigging lines and the method of opening was liable to cause the canopy to tangle in the rigging lines. The apparatus worked perfectly well as an emergency 'chute when manually operated.

Within a week Raymond Quilter had produced a new packing-bag for the Irvin type in which the rigging lines of the parachute were withdrawn from the bag *before* the canopy. The new design was thus a combination of the Irvin parachute with a GQ packing-bag and method of operation. The parachutist now hooked a static-line to a strop attached to a bar running along the roof of the fuselage. The static-line – together with the weight of the man – broke open the bag releasing the rigging lines and canopy once the length of the line was fully extended after the man left the aircraft. The falling body was attached by the harness lift webs to the rigging lines of the parachute canopy and the bag was left dangling on the end of the static-line until pulled in after the drop by the despatcher. The 'X' type, as the new combination was christened, was with further modifications the most successful and popular of the war-time parachutes and continued in service after the war.

The system at Ringway appeared to be working at a price but more temporary problems occurred when a man – who survived – was caught up in the tail wheel of a Whitley, and the bar holding the strops came away during a trial drop with dummies. In August Trooper Watts of the Household Cavalry crashed to his death when his parachute failed to function. No 2 Commando raised by Lieutenant-Colonel C. I. A. Jackson contained a tough breed of men drawn from many regiments. They were volunteers as indeed were all the British servicemen who passed through Ringway and the overseas parachute schools in the war years. Nevertheless not all could face the ordeal of parachuting. After the first two months at Ringway twenty-one officers and 321 other ranks had taken the course. Of this number thirty refused to jump, two were dead and fifteen were too badly injured to carry on.

The Central Landing Establishment formed three sub-units: the Parachute Squadron, the Glider Squadron, and the Technical Development Unit. The nucleus of the experimental glider squadron sprang from a Special Duty Flight at Christchurch. Gliders were needed for several reasons. The RAF in 1940 possessed no transport planes at all suitable for air supply or as troop carriers. The amount of battle equipment and the number of men that a converted bomber such as the Whitley could drop by parachute were obviously limited. As the Germans and the Russians had already demonstrated, air-landed infantry along with ancillary support troops were an integral element of airborne operations. Gliders must now be designed to carry weapons, equipment and troop reinforcements. No such military flying machine existed in Britain when the first 400 prototype Hotspurs were soon ordered by the Ministry for Aircraft Production.

The Air Ministry's lack of interest in airtrooping and military support logistics can be explained in the light of British defence policy after the fall of France. Britain stood with her back to the wall and, as her Army was virtually disarmed, relied entirely on the Air Force and Navy for the defence of the realm. The RAF braced its muscles in an aggressive posture: strategic bomber strikes providing the best means of defence; fighters being essential to protect the bombers and shoot down enemy intruders. The air planners needed the whole of Britain's aircraft resources to implement this policy. In fact although Nos 38 and 46 Groups were as the tide turned assigned to lift Britain's airborne divisions in training and on operations, the RAF throughout the war never really saw itself in the transport rôle.

So the Air Ministry in 1940 would only let the Central Landing Establishment have six old Whitley bombers. Some measure of the difficulties that faced Sir Nigel Norman and John Rock in planning the future of

Winston Churchill reviewing No 11 Special Air Service Battalion in early 1941. Group Captain L. G. Harvey is seen on the PM's right. The troops are dressed in the original combat jacket, which was similar to the *Fallschirmjäger's* smock.

airborne forces may be deduced by simple mathematics. Even if a bomber larger in capacity than the Whitley was converted, perhaps, to carry twenty parachutists, six aircraft would be needed to lift a rifle company. An airborne division similar in establishment to the war-time infantry division would – with no provision for equipment – require nearly 900 aircraft. In Holland the *Luftlandekorps* had achieved their objectives against gallant but negligible opposition and under conditions of complete air superiority. How Britain was to provide air transport and adequate fighter protection on operations for more than one Commando group seemed an impossible question to answer in the bleak winter of 1940–41.

On the development side (now) Lieutenant-Colonel Rock experimented ceaselessly with suitable wearing apparel and supply apparatus. The Commandos undergoing airborne training were given all kinds of protective clothing and equipment such as helmets, tunics, smocks, ponchos, athletic supporters, gloves, knee protectors, elastic ankle bands, long jump boots and respirators. A careful study had obviously been made in respect of the gear worn by Russian and German paratroopers. Early British helmets included a black balaclava-style pilot's helmet, a canvas hood and a flat-topped canvas hat filled with foam rubber. None afforded protection against shrapnel in action but the latter designed in several ways was adopted for training and by the jumping instructors. A long grey-green cotton duck jacket with shoulder straps was worn as combat clothing before the Denison smock was introduced in 1941 as the British paratrooper's camouflage combat smock.

The respirator, which later in the war was discarded as an essential item of equipment, was carried across the chest on a jump and the pockets of the combat jacket and trousers were well filled with items of weaponry such as grenades and spare magazines. The Thompson sub-machine-gun then on issue to the Commandos was for a descent also placed across the chest but inside the upper straps of the parachute harness. A pistol was conveniently stowed inside the jacket. Special kit bags and valises were tried out for personal and specialist equipment such as the radio and for rifles and Bren light machine-guns. For heavier supplies trial drops were

Group Captain Maurice Newnham (right) briefs a Polish pilot for a parachute training flight. Newnham was Commandant of No 1 Parachute Training School at Ringway from May 1941 until the end of the war.

made with canvas bags and panniers like wicker laundry baskets. The Germans used a bomb-shaped container dropped by parachute from the bomb bay of the Ju 52. A similar British bombcell made of sheet metal was produced. The bombcell container was hinged to form two adjacent parts, approximately $4\frac{1}{2}$ feet in length, and could be fitted to any aircraft with a universal bomb rack.

On 21st November the parachute and glider squadrons lost their Commando identity when they were reformed as Wings of No 11 Special Air Service Battalion. The title of this battalion incidentally is not to be confused with that of 'L' Detachment Special Air Service (SAS) founded in August 1941 by Captain David Stirling in the Middle East. David Stirling's original group of seven officers and sixty men, all trained parachutists, was conceived as a desert raiding force and later inducted into the order of battle as the Special Air Service Regiment. No 11 SAS, on the other hand, in September 1941 contributed the nucleus of Brigadier Richard N. Gale's 1st Parachute Brigade and was entitled at that time 1st Parachute Battalion. As 1940 came to a close an operational plan was hatched to implement Churchill's 'butcher and bolt' Commando policy: try out the airborne method in harsh reality; and raise the morale of the restless No 11 SAS Battalion.

The operation that was planned to test the new airborne arm was to be the destruction of an aqueduct in the west-coast province of Campania in southern Italy. The Tragino aqueduct spanned a small stream of that name in sparsely populated country south-east of Salerno not far from the mouth of the River Sele. Ports on the far side of the mainland along the Italian heel were working at high pressure supplying Italian forces in Libya and Cyrenaica. The pipeline ran from the River Sele through the Apennines to the east-coast province of Apulia. Two million Apulian inhabitants, who lived for the most part in Taranto, Brindisi and Bari, depended on the pipeline for their regular water supply. If the local people were temporarily deprived of water, it would be enough, it was thought, to create panic and alarm and have some effect on the Italian war effort.

When one day in January 1941 the commanding officer assembled No 11

Fallschirmjäger manning a belt-fed MG 42 in Crete in May 1941. General Student made devastating use of his parachute and air-lifted battalions during 1940–41 but Crete was the graveyard of German airborne troops.

SAS and asked for volunteers for the raid, every man on parade stepped forward. Major T. A. G. Pritchard, Royal Welch Fusiliers, was chosen to command 'X' troop which included a demolition team and three Italian interpreters. The training of the party of fifty officers and men was supervised by Sir Nigel Norman and John Rock. A mock-up of the aqueduct was erected at Tatton Park and the RAF and Army instructors worked day and night to train the soldiers for the expedition. The Air Ministry was persuaded to release eight more Whitleys, which were quickly converted to the parachute rôle. On 7th February 'X' Troop emplaned at Mildenhall in Suffolk and took off for Malta.

2. Training and Organisation

Airborne training throughout 1941 was empirical but the year ended with a more positive set of rules. Tactical exercises were planned and conducted under simulated battle conditions and the Whitleys made demonstration drops in various parts of the United Kingdom. The first semi-public appearance by British parachutists had taken place the previous December in conjunction with an exercise on Salisbury Plain. Thirty-two men had on that occasion been dropped in sections of eight from two Whitleys each flying two lifts.

On a cold Saturday in April Winston Churchill accompanied by Mrs Churchill, Averill Harriman and senior Army and Air Force officers arrived at Ringway to learn at first hand about the progress being made at the training school. At that time some 400 men were semi-trained as paratroopers but only a few pupils had learned to fly in gliders. The demonstration that had been arranged for the distinguished visitors was to consist of a mock attack on the airfield by forty men jumping from five Whitleys. Five single-seater civilian gliders were also to fly in as part of the show. Wing Commander Norman handed the Prime Minister a radio telephone and invited him to give the formation leader the order to start up. As it happened Churchill declined the offer but the reply that was received after Norman himself gave the instruction was loud enough for all to hear. 'No, I'm not ready to take off – five of the blighters have fainted.'

After the fly-in and drop were completed Harvey, Norman, Strange and

Airborne personalities: (left to right) Brigadier Richard N. Gale, Wing Commander Sir Nigel St V. Norman Bart, Group Captain L. G. Harvey, Lieutenant-Colonel Eric Down ('Charlie Orange') and Major Tim Hope-Thomson (later CO of 4th Parachute Battalion).

Parachutists wearing the black, balaclava-style, leather flying helmet. This headgear was replaced in 1941 by the foam rubber helmet.

Rock were much relieved when Churchill joined them in an enthusiastic discussion on the future of airborne forces. The various objections raised by both the Air Ministry and the War Office had meant that much time had been lost. *Just* how much time was emphasised at 05.30 hours on the morning of 20th May when German bombers started attacking Allied positions along the north coast of the Mediterranean island of Crete. *Generaloberst* Student had at his disposal for the airborne invasion of the island over 500 Junkers transport planes, seventy-five gliders, and some 600 bombers, dive bombers and fighters. 22,750 men of *Fliegerdivision 7* and a mountain division were landed from the air by parachute, in gliders and in transport planes. The successful German invasion of Crete ranks as the only truly strategic operation involving parachute forces attempted in the Second World War. 6,000 Germans were, however, killed and 151 Ju 52s totally destroyed.

As the last shots were being fired in the Battle of Crete, Winston Churchill penned on 27th May another of his characteristic letters to General Lord Ismay. In the letter the Prime Minister wrote: 'This is a sad story [about British parachute troops and gliders], and I feel myself greatly to blame for allowing myself to be overborne by the resistances which were offered. One can see how wrongly based these resistances were when we read the Air Staff paper in the light of what is happening in Crete, and may soon be happening in Cyprus and in Syria . . . We ought to have an Airborne Division on the German model, with any improvements which might suggest themselves from experience. We ought also to have a number of carrier aircraft.'

Paradoxically the immense cost in human life of the Cretan landings meant – on Hitler's orders – the end of the *Fallschirmjäger* in their true rôle. In Britain though events now moved swiftly in the organisation of parachute and glider forces. Four days after Churchill's letter, the Joint Chiefs of Staff approved an Army-RAF proposal to form two parachute brigades, one in the United Kingdom and one in the Middle East, and a glider force sufficient to lift 10,000 men and essential equipment. Altogether some ten medium bomber squadrons were to be converted for parachuting and as glider tugs. So far the airborne only had the eight-seat Hotspur glider for training purposes. Two operational types were put into production: the Horsa, a twenty-five-seater with a payload of nearly three tons; and the Hamilcar, a forty-seater or more importantly a cargo carrier with a seven-ton payload.

During June Lieutenant-Colonel Eric Down was appointed as the commanding officer of No 11 SAS Battalion. The new colonel set a brisk pace in physical fitness and combat training: his ruthless and uncompromising manner earning him the sobriquet 'Dracula'; but before long he was more affectionately known as 'Charlie Orange' (CO). In September the unit was formally mustered as 1st Parachute Battalion at Hardwick near Chesterfield in Derbyshire. At Hardwick Brigadier R. N. Gale OBE, MC, was forming 1st Parachute Brigade. His brigade was – as was the custom in the infantry – to consist of three rifle battalions. Gale decided to keep Down's battalion in one piece and raised the 2nd Battalion (Flavell) and the 3rd Battalion (Lathbury) from new parachute volunteers. Hope-Thompson's 4th Battalion was at first also a part of 1st Parachute Brigade.

A separate headquarters was set up in London at St James's Palace to supervise and coordinate development and training and to lay down the framework of an airborne division. On 29th October Brigadier F. A. M. 'Boy' Browning DSO, then commanding the 24th Guards Brigade, was selected as 'Commander Para-troops and Airborne Troops' with the rank of major-general. The divisional establishment that was envisaged was to be similar in pattern to the British three-brigade infantry division but with a reduced scale of support and service units. The structure of the division was to embrace parachute and air-landed infantry and ancillary arms. 2nd Parachute Brigade was not in being for another ten months but arrangements were immediately made to allocate four infantry battalions to the glider rôle.

1st (Air-Landing) Brigade Group as the new gliderborne formation was called was at first commanded by Brigadier G. F. Hopkinson and consisted of 1st Bn the Border Regiment, 2nd Bn the South Staffordshire Regiment, 2nd Bn the Oxfordshire and Buckinghamshire Light Infantry, 1st Bn the Royal Ulster Rifles, a reconnaissance company, an anti-tank battery and other Brigade units. The glider troops, who were not actually volunteers, were trained separately from the parachute troops. The Army now called for men willing to fly as glider pilots. The Royal Air Force was prepared to give elementary flying instruction but was anxious that the pupils should be soldiers. At the end of 1941 the Glider Pilot Regiment was formed as part of the new Army Air Corps.

A vigorous recruiting drive was organised throughout the Army on behalf of the new airborne battalions. As was the case with the Commandos, many of the commanding officers approached were reluctant to release their best officers and NCOs. A rule was accordingly made that

The Army Air Corps cap badge. The AAC was formally established in December 1941.

THE AIRBORNE FORCES OF THE BRITISH ARMY CONSIST OF PARACHUTE TROOPS AND GLIDER-BORNE TROOPS OF ALL ARMS OF THE SERVICE.

Officers and men in any Regiment or Corps (except R.A.C.), who are medically fit, may apply for transfer to a parachute or glider-borne unit of the Airborne Forces. Additional pay is granted to the Airborne Forces at the rate of 2/- per day for parachute troops, and 1/- per day for glider-borne troops. A limited number of officers and other ranks are urgently required for training as glider-pilots.

Applications for transfer or further information should be made to unit headquarters. Conditions of service are laid down in the following A.C.Is.—1677 of 1941, 275 & 1490 of 1942.

1942. The call for volunteers.

no more than ten volunteers should be taken at one time from a unit in training. The Army jumping instructors, who had outnumbered their RAF colleagues at Ringway, were now transferred as PT instructors to Hardwick. Hardwick Hall, the headquarters of the embryonic 1st Parachute Brigade, was to function as the Airborne Forces Depot for the duration of the war. A selection course was introduced to ensure that only the toughest and most resilient troops were sent on to the Parachute Training School.

The methods used at Hardwick Hall were harsh by any infantry standards. Although the recruit officers and other ranks did not mess together, there was only one set of rules for passing the course. The troops were engaged for a fortnight in intensive physical tests, which can summarily be described as gymnasium, assault course and road work. The recruits were organised into small squads each under an instructor. The NCO instructor from the Army Physical Training Corps had all the persuasive qualities of a pugnacious whippet. The recruits passed from one activity to another 'at the double' and supervising course officers and NCOs watched intently for the slightest sign of weakness in the men. The accent was on finding men with that extra stamina and discipline so vital to elite infantry soldiers. Some attempt was made by Army psychiatrists (known familiarly as 'trick cyclists') to sort out unsuitable candidates. The failure rate amongst volunteers was still fairly high and a 'Return to unit' (RTU) order had much the same effect on a soldier's morale as a sentence on an innocent participant in criminal conspiracy.

After the selection course at Hardwick Hall was over the officers and men the parachute battalions really wanted went on to Ringway. The parachute course also lasted a fortnight and during this time the volunteers were required to make two jumps from a captive balloon cage and five more from aircraft. A night jump was included in the programme and at least two of the seven jumps were performed with kit bags. The graduate paratrooper was granted the right to wear wings sewn below the right shoulder title and an additional 2s. a day parachute pay was payable to all ranks. Refusal to jump at any time on the course carried no more disgrace for a soldier than a prompt RTU. A similar refusal by a trained paratrooper after his posting to an airborne unit was a court martial offence.

Group Captain Maurice Newnham DFC was in mid-1941 made Commandant of the Parachute Training School. After the Army instructors left for Hardwick all the parachute jumping instructors (PJIs) were drawn from the Physical Training Branch of the Royal Air Force. Newnham, like Strange and Harvey – both of whom had been transferred to other assignments – was 'a First World War pilot. He made his first jumps at forty-four years of age and purposefully set about his assignment of organising parachuting on a grand scale. The instructors he chose and most of whom continued to serve under him until the war was over were paragons of their trade. The parachute jumping instructors set always exemplary standards of courage, fitness and skill in supervising the ground and air training of the soldiers in their care.

The men of No 11 SAS Battalion were not alone as parachute volunteers at Ringway. The heterogeneous forces under RAF instruction in 1941 embraced men from Poland, Czechoslovakia, Norway, France, Belgium, Holland and even Germany, Italy and Spain. The largest single foreign element was contributed by the survivors of the Polish Army who had rallied in Britain under General Sikorski after the fall of France. In February 1941 Colonel Stanislaw Sosabowski was allowed to send twenty Polish officers from his unit employed on coast defence in Scotland to the Parachute Training School. Sosabowski, who in September 1939 had led the Infantry Garrison of Warsaw, had only one ambition and that was to return to his beloved Warsaw. He saw a means of doing so in the formation of his own parachute forces. The Independent Polish Parachute Brigade thus came into being and was centred on the Fife coast at Leven. Synthetic training was organised at the ingeniously constructed 'Monkey Grove' where the troops were put through their paces on a pre-Ringway course. Stanislaw Sosabowski did not wait for volunteers to make up his numbers. 'Why,' he asked rhetorically, 'should only the brave die?'

The majority of the Special Operations Executive (SOE) were also parachute-trained at Ringway before embarking on their intelligence and espionage missions in foreign lands. Operational landing zones chosen for these agents – who usually operated in conjunction with resistance groups – would seldom have satisfied Air Force safety requirements for dropping airborne troops. If necessary SOE pupils made practice jumps into hazards such as trees and water and attention was given on their abbreviated parachute course to special methods of carrying equipment. SOE, which came under the overall control of Hugh Dalton as Minister for Economic Warfare, sent some 10,000 British and foreign nationals including about 100 women to the Parachute Training School.

Above.
The training at
Hardwick Hall was
tough by any army's
standards. The
accent was on
physical fitness and
teamwork.

Above right.
PT instructors
demonstrate unarmed
combat techniques.

An intake of potential parachutists at Ringway was organised into syndicates each under an RAF officer assisted by a flight sergeant. A syndicate comprised six sections each of ten men. The term 'stick' was intended to define the number of men who jumped consecutively as a team from an aircraft; 'stick-length' meaning the distance between the first and last man to land on the ground. Each stick was placed under a PJI sergeant who was responsible for all aspects of the ground and air training of the section. The stick of ten men was actually equivalent in size to an infantry section: the stick size increased, however, with aircraft capacity; the American 'lend-lease' Dakota lifting a stick of 24–28 paratroopers.

Synthetic ground training apparatus was built into the airfield hangars and erected nearby in surrounding areas. 'Kilkenny's Circus' was named after Flight-Lieutenant (later Wing Commander) J. C. Kilkenny, the officer in charge of ground training. This complex of training aids was designed to test airborne aptitude and develop proper aircraft drills and parachuting techniques. The men practised landing drills by standing on mats and rolling over from the attention position followed by jumping from benches and sliding down chutes. Instruction in combined flight and landing drills was given to pupils jumping in fixed harnesses on to mats from various swing and platform appliances and constructions of up to about fifteen feet in height. The first test of nerve came when the pupil stood on the 'Fan', which was situated twenty-five feet up a hangar wall. The 'Fan' was a narrow platform from which a pupil stepped off supported by a harness fastened to a length of steel cable wound around a drum. As the man fell so two fans caused an airbrake that controlled the speed of descent.

Fuselages of Whitleys, and later of Halifaxes and Dakotas, were erected for simulated training in correct pre-jump and exit procedures and techniques. Exits from the British converted bombers, pressed into service, including the Stirling, were throughout the war almost always made 'through the hole'. The hole came in different shapes and sizes according to the aircraft. The Albemarle exit, for example, was coffin-shaped and larger than the Whitley hole. Exits from the American Douglas Dakota C-47, in British service from 1942 onwards, were made from the door.

1

2

3

4

5

Kilkenny's Circus. Synthetic training at Ringway. 1) An instructor makes a backward roll. 2) Springboard jump. 3) 'Elbows in and feet and knees together.' 4) The swinging trapeze gives the pupil some idea of parachute oscillation on approaching the ground. 5) Swift disengagement from a parachute harness on hitting the ground is essential. The soldier on the matting is getting the message.

The Polish Brigade built a 100-ft tower made of steel girders at the 'Monkey Grove' as the *pièce de résistance* of their preliminary training course. This idea and many others were later copied or adapted for use by the Parachute Training School. A long steel arm protruded from the top of the tower. A silk parachute canopy, stretched across a large iron hoop, was hung by cable at the end of the arm. The pupil climbed the ladder to the top of the tower, put on the parachute harness and braced himself for the descent. After the command 'Go' the man found himself suspended in thin air beneath the canopy until, at the press of a button, the cable ran out and he floated to the ground.

Towards the end of the first week at Ringway the pupils made their first jumps from a balloon cage winched mechanically by cable from a mobile truck up to 700 feet in the air. A balloon was tried out by instructors in 1940 at the RAF Balloon Development Establishment at Cardington purely as an expedient to relieve the workload on the Whitleys but the First World War relic was and still is accepted as an invaluable instrument of parachute training. Apart from the obvious saving in time and expense, the captive balloon offered several genuine training advantages. The pupil experienced a more powerful sensation of height than when flying in an aircraft and the absence of slipstream and engine noise enabled him to concentrate on his descent, and on amplified ground instructions, right from the start.

The balloon was raised in misty weather and at night if aircraft flying was impracticable but balloon descents were not permitted in wind speeds exceeding seven mph. The cage itself was of simple wooden and metal construction with a canvas covering. For the ascent four pupils crouched around the hole in the centre of the floor. The enormous bag was given to swaying clumsily as it climbed through different air currents and the cage rocked and tilted causing the incumbents to cling desperately to metal bars to prevent untimely exits. An awesome silence and a welcome measure of stability ensued when the grinding of the winch ceased and the balloon at last reached its destination.

Before a jump the small pack normally carried on the back of the shoulders was hung forwards from the neck or strapped to the leg, and the webbing belt supported ammunition pouches and other items of personal equipment. A sleeveless cotton jacket was buttoned over the protruding equipment and the parachute pack and harness were strapped over the jacket which was discarded after the jump. The straps were tightly but comfortably adjusted so that the top of the pack was squarely in line with the shoulder blades. Two upper straps and two leg straps, the latter passing under the crutch, clipped together above the stomach in a safety box fastened to one of the upper straps. Prior to emplaning the stick commander inspected his section and checked that straps were correctly adusted. He gave the circular disc that operated the box a sharp knock to ensure that it was closed.

On climbing into the aircraft the cumbersome gear carried by the paratrooper caused a few swear words. Each man was of necessity lumbered on a drop with a kit bag, Bren or rifle valise. The airborne kit bag was originally designed to take contents weighing up to 100 lbs but 60 lbs was considered a heavy load. The kit bag, which was attached by rope by means

Ground training.
Practice in pulling
in an inflated canopy.
Right. An SAS
recruit jumps from
a lorry moving
at thirty mph.
The scene is the
parachute training
school at Kabrit on
the shore of the
Great Bitter Lake in
Egypt.

of a sleeve to the lower right harness strap, was secured also by an ankle strap to the right leg. The 20-ft length of rope was stowed in an exterior pocket of the kit bag and paid out when the bag was released in flight by jerking out a pin on a cord attachment from the ankle strap. A spring device absorbed the shock of the release of the heavy bag. The Bren and rifle valises, clutched to the body on exit, were attached to the harness in the same way and also released from the ankle strap.

The equipment was not fastened to the body until the order was received to 'prepare for action': the roar of the aircraft engine prevented all but the briefest exchanges in conversation during the approach to the dropping zone; orders were difficult to hear and the unlit interior of a fuselage at night-time added a note of Valkyrian gloom. Aircraft drill depended on the size and layout of the fuselage and the method of exit but the general routine was always the same. After 'hook up' and 'prepare for action', the No 1 as stick commander was responsible for last minute briefing and equipment checks. The aircraft on descending to the prescribed dropping height and on reducing speed for the run-in was liable to lurch and sway. On the red light signal and 'action stations', No 1 moved into the exit hole or door under the watchful eye of the despatcher and was closely followed up by the remainder of the stick. When the green light signalled 'Go' the departures through hole or door were similarly made in an upright posture; the stick pushing off each man in turn feet first from the door of the Dakota, as a contrast to the German scheme of debouching from the Ju 52 head and arms first into the slipstream.

Descents were accomplished at aircraft speeds of between 100–120 mph; an exception to this rule was made for the Hudson, flown for the most part from overseas stations, which could not safely reduce to this speed. In training a ceiling of 700 feet was maintained and jumping was not allowed in wind speeds exceeding 15 mph. Special circumstances enforced lower operational dropping heights to prevent the widespread dispersion of the troops and their equipment on the ground. The distance between the first and last man on the ground of a quick Whitley ten-man

General Sir Bernard Paget talks to a parachute jumping instructor at Ringway. Air Marshal Sir Arthur Barratt is in the centre and Group Captain Maurice Newnham on the extreme right.

Left.
Ready for a jump.
Right.
'Up seven hundred feet – four men jumping.' Four static-lines can be seen attached to the short, horizontal bar of the balloon cage. The instructor is standing in the rear.

A busy day at Tatton Park.

stick could amount even in favourable conditions to 500–600 yards. The bombcell containers were released in the middle of a stick. In the ten-man stick, for example, an essential pause was created when No 5 operated the switch of the electrical bomb-dropping mechanism ('Mickey Mouse') before making his exit.

At first the Ringway instructors knew very little about methods of controlling and guiding a parachute in flight. When a parachute canopy is fully developed the parachutist looks up and discovers that he is suspended from two harness buckles on the shoulders by four, three-foot webbing straps (lift webs), each of which is attached by a metal ring to seven rigging lines rising twenty-five feet upwards to the periphery and into the fabric of the canopy. The man is able to reach up and grasp two of the four lift webs, two of which incline forwards and two backwards from the shoulder buckles. An appreciable degree of flight control can be achieved by pulling down at the right time on either one or two of the appropriate straps. But there is always a first time for discovering the principle of a thing!

The exhortation that accompanied the parachutist from training school to distant battlefield was 'keep your arms and elbows in and feet and knees together.' The reason for the precept was to teach him to absorb the landing

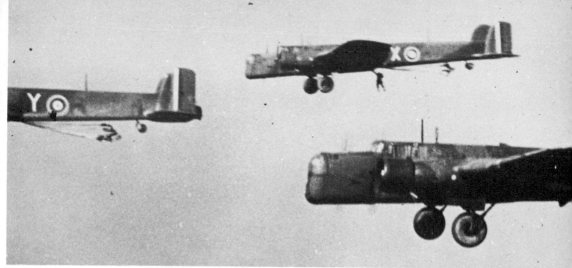

Top
Whitleys over the
dropping zone.
Empty parachute
bags can be seen
trailing beneath the
leading aircraft.

Left
An officer makes a
model exit from a
balloon cage.

Right.
A DZ officer gives
advice to a
parachutist.

Below
A gust of wind has
filled his canopy but
this man has a firm
grip on the lift webs.

shock by spreading the loads over a large area of his body, instead of taking them all on the soles of his feet. A truly vertical descent at a speed that permitted him to land feet first and withstand the shock by flexing his legs was rare. More often he floated in at the mercy of a horizontal wind or gust and swinging moreover from his parachute like the pendulum of a clock. Consequently he was taught to touch down in the line of drift, distributing the shock of impact between the combined strength of both legs and on one side of the body by rolling on to the ground from the feet, through the thigh and hip to the shoulder.

Until good parachuting styles were perfected by the instructors, pupils at Ringway attempted only forward rolls on landing; and in order to reduce the risk of an uncontrolled backward landing, they were told to turn about in the harness by crossing the front lift webs and go in 'forwards'. Flight-Lieutenant Julian Gebolys, the senior Polish instructor, was a pioneer in developing the art of arresting the speed, drift and oscillation of a parachute. A new flight technique was introduced after the discovery that the shape of the canopy could be altered like the sail of a ship and resistance to wind currents increased by pulling down on either one or two of the lift webs. A fast forward drift was corrected by manipulating the back lift webs and *vice versa*. Control was exercised over forward, sideways and backward movements: the angle of approach to the ground was expressed in terms of 'forward-left or right', 'side-left or right', or 'back-left or right'; but a backward landing still meant turning the body into the line of drift.

The effect of the slipstream on the parachutist was modified by the drag of the static-line and, if a good exit was achieved, he was whisked past the tail of the aircraft as if supported by divine providence. His canopy was in fact open before much vertical height was lost and he had adequate time to go through his drills before adopting a good parachuting position. This drill sequence was to 'look up' and see if the canopy had opened normally; turn about in the harness and make all-round observation; and take evasive action if floating on a collision course with another parachutist or a container. (The problem of collision was exacerbated when sticks jumped from both port and starboard doors of an aircraft, but British troops had little experience of this practice until after the war.) The kit bag and weapons valises were released when the way was clear below and fortuitously lessened the shock of landing for the parachutists. The average force of impact on landing can be compared to the shock of leaping from a 12-ft wall. Swift disengagement from the harness straps on the ground was advisable as the possibility of dragging accrued if the wind inflated the canopy. For landing in trees the parachutist was taught to safeguard his face. The technique for landing in water demanded complete release from the parachute harness before entering the water.

Fatalities and severe injuries could usually be attributed to the same recurrent causes. The surest way of preventing an accident whether jumping through the hole or the door was to hold the body stiffly at attention. If the body entered into the slipstream at any other angle or worse somersaulted forwards the rigging lines inevitably twisted together. This meant that the front and back sets of rigging lines were interwoven above the lift webs in two strands like a thick rope. As the development of the parachute was

restricted so the rate of fall was increased and no flight control was possible until the twists were eliminated. The blown periphery or 'thrown line' was another cause of a dangerously fast descent. This abnormality was formed when part of the periphery was firstly blown inwards and then outwards through the rigging lines producing a secondary inverted canopy. Another manifestation of the blown periphery was experienced when a portion of the canopy blew between two rigging lines and the tendency ensued for the canopy to roll up at the skirt. A 'streamer' was the name given to a parachute canopy that paid out but failed to develop until the last moment. The 'roman candle', the most feared of the freak conditions, was the kind of 'streamer' that failed to open at all.

The servicing and packing of parachutes at Ringway after 1941 was the job of the Women's Auxiliary Air Force. Over 400,000 drops were mounted from the airfield during the war and only one fatal accident was traced to faulty packing. The girls worked as a team under a flight-sergeant and were constantly reminded of their onerous duties in their place of work by a large sign bearing the following words: REMEMBER A MAN'S LIFE DEPENDS ON EVERY PARACHUTE YOU PACK. The efficiency and dedication of the WAAF packers contributed immensely to the confidence so prominently displayed by parachute troops in training and in battle.

In March 1942 1st Parachute Brigade moved out from the Hardwick depot (officially opened in April) to Bulford Camp on the Salisbury Plain. Brigadier Gale had already been transferred from the brigade to the War Office where he worked temporarily in a newly created airborne post as

Mock battle. 1st Parachute Brigade shortly before embarking for North Africa.

Above
Major-General K. N. Crawford takes the plunge. The parachute jumping instructors of No 1 Parachute Training School often carried out experimental water jumps at Rostherne Mere. Here the Director of Staff Duties Air, War Office, makes a guest appearance.

Right.
1st Parachute Battalion at Ringway in October 1941. The men are armed with Tommy guns. Two of the soldiers in the background are from the Polish Brigade.

Director of Staff Duties Air. Brigadier E. W. C. Flavell MC, promoted from the 2nd Battalion, was the new brigade commander. General Browning's 1st Airborne Division was slowly taking shape in the Bulford area; his headquarters being situated at Syrencot House in Figheldean.

No 38 Wing of the Royal Air Force, the new air transport arm, was in business in February at RAF Netheravon under Group Captain Sir Nigel Norman and was already actively cooperating with a few glider pilots and units of Hopkinson's 1st (Air-Landing) Brigade Group. The Army and the Air Force together faced an ambitious programme of expansion. So far no one had actually thought of an operational philosophy for the employment of parachute and gliderborne troops. The Army must, of course, be ready to take on anything and the Air Force meantime keep pace with the mounting need for carrier and tug aircraft. But the airborne division now had a problem of recruitment to solve.

Since the original Commando group had converted as No 11 SAS Battalion, the appeal for parachute volunteers had ranged far and wide throughout the British Army. Even so the War Office offer of extra duty pay was not greeted with widespread enthusiasm for what was involved and the rate at which suitable men were passing through Hardwick was disappointing. A new recruitment policy was implemented in the circumstances after a decision to draft trained infantry battalions to the Airborne Forces Depot and submit them *in toto* to the rigours of the selection course. The new plan worked well. The new battalions drawn from famous county regiments brought their own regimental traditions and comradeship based on pride of locality to a fledgling regiment. Those individuals who did not step forward or failed the course were replaced by volunteers from other sources. The first two regiments to provide battalions for conversion were the Queen's Own Cameron Highlanders and the Royal Welch Fusiliers. The 7th Battalion of the former and the 10th Battalion of the latter became the 5th (Scottish) and 6th (Royal Welch) Parachute Battalions respectively. The Camerons as was the privilege of a Scottish regiment brought their own pipe band. The 4th (later the 'Wessex')

Battalion was transferred from 1st Parachute Brigade and on 17th July 1942 Brigadier Eric Down formed 2nd Parachute Brigade from the 4th, 5th and 6th Battalions.

The parachute forces had grown steadily but in terms of identity at least were still a maverick breed. General Browning created a more positive image for his men when in mid-1942 he chose the maroon beret as the distinctive headgear of the airborne division and the emblem of Bellerophon mounted on the winged horse Pegasus was now worn on the arm of all airborne soldiers. The time had come, however, for the existence of parachute troops to be formally sponsored in life by legitimate parenthood. The 'Regiment' in peace-time infantry of the line is the proud parent of two battalions [1st and 2nd]; but in time of war the number is extended to include serving Territorial and conscript battalions. The parachute battalions had no parent regiment or corps until on 1st August 1942 the matter was rectified and the War Office approved the formation of the Parachute Regiment to serve in conjunction with the Glider Pilot Regiment as part of the Army Air Corps.

Major-General F. A. M. Browning DSO, educated at Eton and Sandhurst, was forty-six years of age in 1942. He was commissioned in the Grenadier Guards in 1915 and a few months later was in the fighting line in France and, before his twentieth birthday, he had won the Distinguished Service Order and the French Croix de Guerre. Between the wars Browning's career was that of a regimental officer except for four years when he was Adjutant at the Royal Military Academy, Sandhurst. In 1939 he was commanding officer of 2nd Bn the Grenadier Guards and was subsequently Commandant of the Small Arms School, Netheravon, Commander of 128th Infantry Brigade, and Commander of the 24th Independent Guards Brigade Group. In his younger days he was a champion athlete, a bob sleigh enthusiast, and he represented England in the high hurdles at the Olympic Games.

The general was known universally as 'General Boy' or 'Boy' Browning and he was endowed with the groomed looks of a cinema star of the 1930s. Not a few of the top military commanders of the Second World War were noted for irregularities, subtle or otherwise, of service uniform. 'Boy' Browning's own personal eccentricities in this respect erred strongly in favour of sartorial perfection, and in the matter of turn-out he was held in complete awe by all who met him. Lieutenant-General Sir Frederick Browning GCVO, KBE, CB, DSO, to give him his definitive title when he died in 1965, married in 1932 Daphne du Maurier, the novelist, and it is said that the association of the spirit of airborne forces with the Greek legend of Bellerophon can be traced to the influence of Lady Browning.

General Browning was greatly respected for his immense skill and drive in welding the airborne units together as integral fighting formations. Two airborne divisions, the 1st and in 1943 the 6th, were raised in Britain and in April 1943 Browning received the title of Major-General Airborne Forces. The 'division' in the British Army is the smallest formation to go into action with an adequate scale of support and service units. The bulk of the fighting strength of a conventional infantry division, which in 1942 numbered 757 officers and 16,764 men, was contained in two infantry brigades, each of three rifle battalions, and a tank brigade. The principal supporting arm was that of the artillery comprising three field regiments, an anti-tank regiment and a light anti-aircraft regiment. Other support elements included the Royal Engineers, Divisional Signals and a reconnaissance regiment. The service elements were represented by the Royal Army Service Corps (transport), Royal Army Medical Corps, Royal Army Ordnance Corps and Provost as well as other minor units manned by the engineers. At the head of the division the headquarters staff was assisted by intelligence, field security and defence sections. The airborne forces divisional establishment was to follow the same overall pattern, the tank brigade being replaced by the air-landing brigade, but the drastic cut in ancillary services that was necessary to achieve air mobility amounted to a reduction in strength of about one-third as compared with the conventional infantry division.

A rifle battalion numbering 600–800 all ranks was considered appropriate to the function of the Parachute Regiment but the title 'rifle' in the airborne case is misleading since the parachute troops carried more sub-machine-guns and pistols than rifles. A parachute battalion deployed usually three but sometimes four companies each totalling five officers and 120 men plus Battalion HQ and HQ Company: the company was divided up into Company HQ and three thirty-six-man platoons each commanded by an officer; and the platoon in turn was arranged under Platoon HQ in three ten-man sections led by non-commissioned officers.

The fire power of the battalion – without assistance from outside sources – lay with an assortment of weapons: the hand grenade, sub-machine-gun, pistol, rifle, Bren light machine-gun, PIAT (Projector Infantry Anti-tank) and 2-in and 3-in mortars. A small proportion of medium machine-guns were also employed. The airborne also made use of the Mills bomb (a form of grenade) and other kinds of explosive weapons such as the Bangalore torpedo and their own Gammon bomb.

Glider pilots. Their helmets were fitted with head sets for communication with tug navigators and base control.

The rôle of the Air-Landing/Glider Brigade, which possessed a heavier scale of infantry equipment, was to reinforce the strength of parachute troops in battle with troops of similar calibre and to fly in such guns, transport, stores and supplies as were essential to the reasonable cover of the parachute brigades on the ground. Each glider battalion numbering up to 976 men consisted of four rifle companies each of four platoons. The airborne troops who travelled in the gliders were not subjected to initial selection procedures but were nonetheless put through intensive infantry training. This hazardous occupation, which some may consider more dangerous than parachuting, was rewarded by the payment of an extra 1s. a day special duty pay for all ranks.

The Glider Pilot Regiment, which was actually formed on 21st December 1941, consisted by August 1942 on paper of two battalions of glider pilots. The 1st Battalion under Lieutenant-Colonel John Rock, who more than any other had earned the title of the pioneer or father of British airborne forces, was at the Tilshead Depot near Devizes. Shortly after qualifying as a glider pilot, John Rock was so severely crushed by sandbags (used on trials in place of troops as ballast) in his glider – on breaking up on a night landing – that he died soon after from his injuries. Lieutenant-Colonel George Chatterton, who now assumed command of the 1st Battalion, was an air enthusiast and former RAF fighter pilot of great experience.

The glider pilot's job was to fly light or heavy gliders filled with soldiers or materials behind tug aircraft in all kinds of weather conditions – and on release of the towrope – to swoop down like a bird by day or night on enemy-held terrain. On landing the glider pilots were expected to fight individually as infantry soldiers or collectively as a combat unit at the disposal of the divisional commander.

A preliminary training cadre drawn from trained Army units was instructed in all facets of infantry skills and elementary flying knowledge at the training depot. Drill instructors strictly enforced the parade ground atmosphere of the Brigade of Guards and glider pilots were in consequence the peers amongst war-time flyers for bearing and turn-out. Aptitude tests assessed physical, psychological and moral fitness for the tasks ahead and the failure rate at this early stage was probably as much as twenty-five per cent. The pilot training in powered aircraft, which lasted from twelve to fourteen weeks, was conducted at the Royal Air Force Elementary Flying Training School at Derby and was common at that stage to both Army and RAF pupils. The glider pilots were awarded wings worn on the left breast after conversion courses from the Hotspur trainers on to the light Horsa gliders flown on operations. By this time the qualified pilots had experienced six months of specialised training and were proficient in day and night flying. The most experienced pilots were chosen to convert on to the heavy-duty Hamilcars.

On take-off the glider was drawn forward by the tug on the ground until the towrope was taut and the two aircraft climbed steadily into the air. The glider pilots were apprised of the height and bearing of their course to the landing zone and at the briefing beforehand had already made a careful study of landmarks *en route* and aerial photographs of the area of destination. During the flight the normal position for the glider was just above or just below the slip-stream of the tug. The precise moment of departure from the tug was chosen by the glider pilot in control and the release mechanism for the towrope was operated from the glider cockpit. (Intercommunication was possible by means of a line wound around the towrope.) On landing in favourable conditions, the glider came quickly to rest within a distance of up to twenty yards from the point of impact. Thus after gliding in at anything from 60–100 mph, the occupants of the glider were in for a rough jolt.

After their flying courses the pilots embarked upon training leading to cooperation with airborne troops at one of the two Glider Operational Training Units established early in 1942 at Netheravon and Kidlington. Group Captain Sir Nigel Norman's HQ No 38 Wing RAF, which was located alongside HQ 1st Airborne Division in Syrencot House at Fighel-dean, controlled – separately from the glider units – two exercise squadrons stationed at the airfield nearby at Netheravon. These tug and paratroop squadrons were named No 296 (Glider Exercise) Squadron and No 297 (Parachute Exercise) Squadron. The Whitley was the principal aircraft employed by both squadrons in 1942 but the Hotspur tug took the anti-quated form of an old biplane called the Hawker Hector.

At first No 38 Wing's general assignment was to lift 1st Airborne Divi-sion on training exercises and to teach Bomber Command pilots how to drop parachute troops and tow gliders. Bomber Command was responsible for supplying aircrew and aircraft as required for operational duties but on expanding No 38 Wing flew its own missions and in the spring of 1944 – as No 38 Group – numbered six Stirling, two Albemarle and two Halifax front-line squadrons. Air Commodore Sir Nigel St V. Norman CBE, Bart, who had served Airborne Forces so well since the parachute school first opened, was sadly killed in a Hudson crash in May 1943. No 38 Group, which dated from 11th October 1943, was commanded by Air Vice-Marshal L. N. Hollinghurst CB, OBE, DFC. The Airborne Forces Establish-ment responsible at Ringway for technical development was reconstituted in February 1942 under Group Captain L. G. Harvey as the Airborne Forces Experimental Establishment. Basic instruction in parachuting remained at Ringway where the unit was known for the rest of the war as No 1 Parachute Training School.

Prior to the invasion of Northern Europe in June 1944 the Glider Pilot Regiment replaced their Army battalion system by two Wings similar in organisation to Air Force practice. Nos 1 and 2 Wings then supported between them nine squadrons, which were further broken down into flights consisting of four officers and forty other ranks. The 'other rank' pilots were usually NCOs of sergeant or staff sergeant rank. The number of flights available in a squadron at any time was flexible. Each glider crew in the flight was teamed up at the home airfield with its respective bomber crew – namely first pilot, second co-pilot, navigator, engineer and gunner. Colonel (later Brigadier) George Chatterton headed the two Glider Wings as Commander Glider Pilots.

Throughout 1942 1st Airborne Division prepared for their impending battles in North Africa, Sicily and Italy. Early in the year Operation 'Biting', a successful attempt to obtain vital information about German radar techniques, was mounted on the night of 27th–28th February by 'C'

Company of 2nd Parachute Battalion against a German radar station situated on the French coast near the village of Bruneval. In November an unsuccessful sortie (Operation 'Freshman'), incurring tragic consequences for the participants, was launched by a small party of gliderborne engineers in an attempt to destroy the Norsk Hydro plant at Vemork some sixty miles due west of Oslo in Norway. The main body of the division spent the summer engaged on airborne exercises involving section and platoon descents with arms containers, night balloon jumps, and tactical exercises increasing as the weeks went by in tempo and unit scale. The strain on RAF Bomber Command and No 38 Wing in particular in providing enough aircraft and specially trained crews to lift the expanding parachute and glider units was greatly relieved by the arrival on the scene of the renowned Dakota transport aircraft of the United States Army Air Force.

The Allied landings in North Africa (Operation 'Torch') were set in motion on 8th November 1942. The invasion forces, mainly American, were to land at eleven points from Casablanca to Algiers. The immediate aim of the Eastern Anglo-American Task Force landing in Algeria was to push eastwards into Tunisia and link up with the British Eighth Army advancing from the Western Desert. General Browning was in September ordered to mobilise 1st Parachute Brigade for airborne operations in North Africa.

1st Airborne Division completed mobilisation by 1st May 1943 and shortly after 2nd Parachute Brigade and 1st (Air-Landing) Brigade sailed for the Middle East to join up with 1st Parachute Brigade. 1st Airborne Division was commanded from May 1943 by Major-General G. F. Hopkinson OBE, MC, who led the British airborne assault in July on the Catania-Syracuse sector in Sicily and later in September in the amphibious landing at Taranto on the Italian mainland.

Orders for the formation of 6th Airborne Division were issued on 3rd May 1943. By this time Brigadier James Hill, who had won the DSO as 1st Bn Commander in Tunisia, had assembled 7th, 8th and 9th Parachute Battalions as 3rd Parachute Brigade. As was now usual these battalions were impressed into the Parachute Regiment on a regional basis as follows: 7th (Light Infantry) Battalion from 10th Bn the Somerset Light Infantry; 8th (Midland) Battalion from 13th Bn the Royal Warwickshire Regiment; 9th (Eastern and Home Counties) Battalion from 10th Bn the Essex Regiment. On 1st June the War Office renamed 10th Bn the Green Howards and 2nd/4th Bn the South Lancashire Regiment as the 12th (Yorkshire) and 13th (Lancashire) Parachute Battalions of Brigadier Nigel Poett's 5th Brigade to partner Hill's 3rd Brigade in 6th Airborne Division.

Major-General Richard Nelson Gale, who formed and on 6th June 1944 led 6th Airborne Division in Normandy, presented the epitome of the popular image of the British senior officer of the Regular Army. A veteran of the First World War, in which he was commissioned in 1915 in the Worcestershire Regiment and served also as a machine-gun officer, his bluff appearance belied his intellectual strength, shrewdness of purpose and mastery of the soldier's trade. Between the wars he had spent long years on the Indian cantonments and was a graduate of the Quetta Staff College. Gale, who invariably wore riding breeches and polished field boots with his Denison smock, arrived on 7th May to assume tenancy of Syrencot House, the red Georgian residence at Figheldean now vacated by 1st Airborne HQ. One of his first divisional orders bore the words: 'Go To It – This motto will be adopted by the 6th Airborne Division and as such should be remembered by all ranks in action against the enemy, in training, and during the day to day routine duties.'

In July the division was joined by the 1st Canadian Parachute Battalion. About 100 Canadian soldiers were originally parachute-trained at Ringway before returning to Canada to develop their own recruitment and training at the Parachute School at Camp Shilo, Manitoba. By the gateway to the camp, an enormous notice bore the message: 'Don't think about women – think about war'; that the advice was in part disregarded is clear from the fact that the walls of the Officers' Club were smothered with pictures of naked girls. The Canadian Battalion was posted to Hill's brigade; the 7th Battalion being transferred out to bring Poett's brigade up to full fighting strength.

On the move to North Africa 1st Airborne Division took along its gunners – 1st Airborne Light Regiment RA – and other support and service units but only two glider battalions. 1st Bn the Border Regiment and 2nd Bn the South Staffordshire Regiment spearheaded the British airborne landings in July on the south-eastern coastline of Sicily. At home the two remaining glider battalions – 2nd Bn the Oxfordshire and Buckinghamshire Light Infantry and 1st Bn the Royal Ulster Rifles – went over to 6th (Air-Landing) Brigade and were in time joined by 12th Bn the Devonshire Regiment. 6th (Air-Landing) Brigade was organised and led by Brigadier the Hon. Hugh Kindersley OBE, MC, Scots Guards. General Gale's artillery was represented by the 53rd (Worcestershire Yeomanry) Air-Landing Light Regiment RA equipped with the American 75-mm howitzers.

The Special Air Service parachute school established by David Stirling in mid-1941 at Kabrit in Egypt was transformed in its early days into an RAF unit called No 4 Middle East Parachute Training School. Brigadier J. W. 'Shan' Hackett's 4th Parachute Brigade began to take shape at Kabrit in November 1942 but before much progress had been made both school and brigade moved to a pleasanter climate at Ramat David near Haifa in northern Palestine. In addition to training new parachute battalions and the SAS, the school, as at Ringway, took on its share of the 'Specials' of many nationalities who dropped in enemy-occupied countries. 'Shan' Hackett's brigade was to consist of 10th, 11th and 151st Parachute Battalions. The nucleus of the 10th (Sussex) Parachute Battalion (formerly 2nd Bn the Royal Sussex Regiment) had fought with distinction as Desert Rats at El Alamein: the 11th was recruited – as was the balance of the 10th – from volunteers serving in units in the Middle East; and the 151st was the original 156th (British) Parachute Battalion transferred from India. The aircraft flown at the school included Vickers Valentias, Bombays, Hudsons and Wellingtons but Dakotas came into general use in 1943. No 4 Middle East Parachute Training School at Ramat David where the practice dropping zone was located in the Vale of Jezreel was moved again as the war progressed to Gioia airfield near Bari in Italy. After the fall of Rome parachute training also took place at the Lido di Roma.

In 1943 few doubts existed at Syrencot House as to the destination in

'Stand to the door!' The parachutist about to jump from the door of a Dakota is carrying a kit bag *and* a weapons valise.

battle of 6th Airborne Division, but the precise nature of its operational rôle in the coming struggle for Europe was by no means certain. The Pyrrhic victory achieved by the parachute and glider units of the British 1st and United States 82nd Airborne Divisions in Sicily in July was painful to contemplate: inadequate training of aircrew, errors in airborne method and tactics, air transport shortages and adverse weather conditions led to near disaster; Colonel (later General) Jim Gavin of the US 505th Parachute Infantry Regiment describing the Allied airborne invasion in plain language as a 'self-adjusting foul-up'.

Many lessons were nevertheless gained from the Sicilian experience. The capture of the two important bridges – Primosole and Ponte Grande, leading respectively to Catania and Syracuse – pointed clearly to a suitable type of objective for Allied airborne forces in North West Europe. Central control of airborne forces, probably by an Air supremo, was advisable. Aircrew and glider pilots needed much more training than hitherto before embarking on operations. Pathfinder techniques were necessary for the

'Green on, Go!' A
training jump in the
Middle East.

The new cap badge
of the Parachute
Regiment was issued
on 25th May 1943.

marking and lay-out of dropping and landing zones by day and night. The concentration of airborne troops in strength on the ground was preferable to the dispersal of battalion areas.

During the advance of an infantry division each new set of circumstances develops from a series of preparatory moves. The infantryman has the opportunity of observing the terrain and his enemy and may even be able to reconnoitre the enemy positions. Intelligence sources and aerial surveillance further enable the commander to make a reasonable assessment of the arrangement and strength of his opponent's dispositions. In the attack the infantry edge forward along a path blasted by their own artillery and tanks and need not fear envelopment if their flanks are protected by fellow infantry and tanks of adjacent divisions in the line.

An airborne division on the other hand in a similar war situation may be taken on a short flight and all concerned from the general and his staff to the infantry section plunged into total encirclement by enemy forces. A major airborne operation is *per se* a demonstration of air power: substantial numbers of carrier aircraft are essential to lift the various units into battle: fighter squadrons are absolutely vital to the protection of the sky armada: air strikes and fighter cover must continue in support of the lodgement on the ground; and re-supply from the air of food and *matériel* be both constant and plentiful. The purpose of seizing and holding a vital objective in the rear of the enemy lines is usually tactical in conception and has the intention of facilitating the advance of the main ground forces. Airborne troops dropped and air-landed into action must therefore be confident of a quick link-up with their 'parent' Army formation.

As military thinking progressed it was realised that an airborne division should *only* be launched into battle in conjunction with a full-scale offensive; and that having secured for the Army commander a safe means of negotiating an oncoming obstacle such as a bridge over a river, the isolated forces confined to their defensive perimeter must expect relief within a few days. An airborne operation of this kind was of course doomed to disaster unless the land attack stood every chance of initial success and poured quickly through the enemy's front-line defences. The argument often put forward, however, that specialist airborne troops were wasted in any other rôle was scarcely practical. The battle plan might call for parachute and glider shock tactics launched as part of an offensive followed for the airborne troops by several months of hard combat as infantry of the line.

Throughout the active months preceding D-Day, Gale and his men were based on the Salisbury Plain but made frequent flying visits to the desolate training areas of Scotland. Exercise 'Pegasus' in June 1943 was the first scheme organised on any scale by the division and included a mock assault on a coastal battery erected for the purpose at Christchurch on the River Avon. 6th Airborne Division soon came into neighbourly contact with American airborne troops and aircrew: the 101st Airborne Division (the 'Screaming Eagles') were stationed at Newbury in Berkshire; and the 9th Troop Carrier Command gave much assistance to No 38 Wing RAF. As the tempo of airborne training increased, No 1 Parachute Training School came under the direct control of 38 Wing and PJIs were attached to the division at Netheravon to organise refresher parachute training and to act as despatchers on exercises. It was actually during this period in late 1943 that jumping with airborne kit bags and valises was first tried out and approved by the RAF instructors.

By November 1943 1st Airborne Division, less 2nd Parachute Brigade, had been withdrawn from Italy and was homeward bound for the United Kingdom. Brigadier C. H. V. Pritchard's 2nd Independent Parachute Brigade Group composed of 4th, 5th and 6th Parachute Battalions and supporting arms remained in the line and advanced with the Eighth Army beyond Rome until briefed in August 1944 for the Allied airborne landings in the South of France. After completing their assignment near St Raphael in Provence, Pritchard's brigade withdrew to Italy and on 12th October 'C' Company of the 4th Battalion provided the nucleus of a small combat group that took off from Brindisi and dropped in Greece on the Megara airfield on the southern coastal road from Corinth to Athens. The rest of the brigade followed closely behind and was involved in the expulsion of the retreating Germans and in the fratricidal fighting and riots that raged for the next three months in Greece.

The veteran 1st Parachute Brigade commanded since the North African campaign by Brigadier Gerald Lathbury DSO, MBE had been joined on the invasion of Italy by 'Shan' Hackett's 4th Parachute Brigade raised in the Middle East. These were the two parachute brigades that finally formed up in England with 'Pip' Hicks' 1st (Air-Landing) Brigade as 1st Airborne Division at the close of 1943. 1st Bn (later No 1 Wing) the Glider Pilot Regiment had in Italy been thrown into the line as infantry and were glad to return to flying gliders. 1st Airborne's glider troops namely 1st Bn the Border Regiment and 2nd Bn the South Staffords were now reinforced by the addition of 7th Bn the King's Own Scottish Borderers.

Command of 1st Airborne Division passed in December 1943 to Major-General R. E. Urquhart DSO, who had earned an excellent reputation leading the Malta Brigade in the invasions of Sicily and Italy. Although there were several able and much experienced parachute brigadiers in the running for the job, General Browning brought in a fresh mind to contend with the problems of managing an elite airborne division. Roy Urquhart, a Scot aged forty-three, had been commissioned in 1920 in the Highland Light Infantry and after passing through the Staff College at Camberley 1936–37 had served in staff appointments in India. Prior to commanding the Malta Brigade, Urquhart had served as GSO 1 51st Highland Division.

1st and 6th Airborne Divisions forming Browning's 1st Airborne Corps were not supposed to be identical in composition but the main features of organisation in respect of both infantry and support and service units were the same. The need to provide aids on the ground to direct aircraft on the DZ/LZs was answered by the services of the Pathfinders of the Independent Parachute Company, whose job it was to be in position shortly before the arrival of the first lift. A simple air-to-ground radio device called Rebecca-Eureka was first employed by airborne forces in November 1942 when Eureka was smuggled into Norway to guide the engineer raiding party to the heavy water plant at Vemork. Rebecca was used by pilots in the war to obtain ground signals from Eureka as a navigational aid as well as for the identification of airborne target zones.

DZ/LZ recognition in good weather by day was comparatively simple but the release of several hundred gliders landing at thirty-second intervals incurred collision risks. A system was accordingly invented to channel the gliders from their release point down through an imaginary funnel to pre-selected positions on the ground perimeter. Basing their calculations at the operational briefing on the distance of glide from the release height, the glider pilots having studied the air photograph picked out ground features as route markers for the glide-in and pin-pointed their individual landing places with a reasonable degree of accuracy. Night operations naturally presented the real location hazards. The most common method of dropping parachutists at night was to fly on to a line marked by two lights each placed several hundred yards apart. If the airmen flew on to the DZ on the correct bearing the green light in the aircraft was switched on – with the troops already at 'action stations' – as the two ground lights appeared at ninety degrees to port and starboard on the line of approach. For the gliders this arrangement was developed into a flarepath laid out in the form of a 'T'; the pathfinder troops placing three electric lights seventy-five yards apart at the head of the landing strip, and five more

Composition of an Airborne Division 1942–45

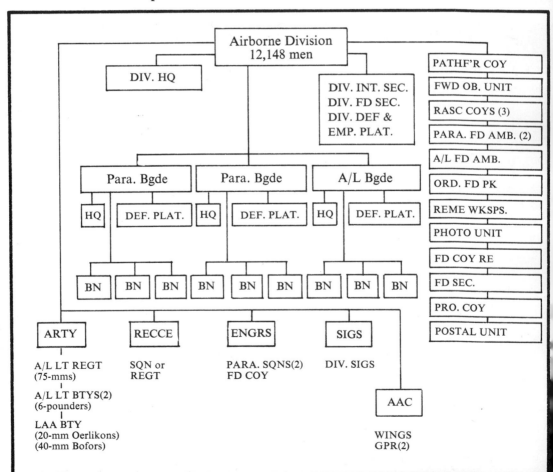

forming the stem fifty yards apart. The lights were masked to shine upwards only and a flashing beacon was positioned three hundred yards from the foot of the flarepath to indicate the release point and entrance to the funnel. (The 'T'-principle with suitable markers could also of course be used by day for LZ identification.)

The divisional artillery comprised the three batteries of the Air-Landing Light Regiment, plus two separate anti-tank batteries and a light anti-aircraft battery. 1st Air-Landing Light Regiment was equipped in the spring of 1943 at Bulford with 3.7–in howitzers but this gun was discarded in favour of the American 75-mm pack howitzer. The 75-mm gun was actually a mountain gun carried by mules but it was pneumatised and proved ideal for transportation in a glider. A typical Horsa gun load included a gun, a jeep, a trailer, one or two motorcycles and six passengers. An airborne battery totalled six guns, and each gun sub-section consisted of a gun, two jeeps and three trailers for the ammunition and stores.

Though confined perforce to a restricted area, an airborne division nonetheless required timely information about enemy dispositions and intentions. The Reconnaissance Regiment allocated by squadron to each brigade was equipped with the pre-war seven-ton Tetrarch tank, jeeps and motor cycles. (At Arnhem 1st Airborne's requirement was reduced to only one squadron equipped with armoured jeeps.) The Hamilcars were in fact invented with the Tetrarch in mind.

Each parachute brigade additionally supported its own squadron of Royal Engineers, and an air-landing brigade its own company. The parachute engineers set up a field park for their engineer stores and performed the usual RE demolition, bridging and field construction tasks. Royal Signals ran the divisional wireless net and kept the external links open with the supporting artillery, air support and re-supply agencies and for long range communication with home bases. Signallers for routine contact used standard British Army radio sets ranging from the 18/68 to 76 sets. The 38 set of 0.5 watt output operating on voice up to a maximum of four miles was the most common means of communication. The divisional unit framework also embraced Ordnance, the Royal Electrical and Mechanical Engineers (REME) workshop, and Provost and Field Security sections.

A parachute field ambulance staffed by nine Royal Army Medical Corps officers and just over one hundred other ranks was attached to each parachute brigade and consisted of an HQ, two surgical teams and four sections. An air-landing field ambulance was constituted on similar lines but carried a slightly larger establishment. Specially designed airborne medical and surgical equipment was conveyed in gliders and dropped in arms containers. In Normandy supplies of blood plasma packed inside arms containers and dropped to the field ambulances enabled surgeons to perform forty operations during the first two days of the invasion.

The Royal Army Service Corps was responsible for air cargoes dropped from aircraft and the war-time air despatch companies were actually born within the framework of airborne forces. (The loading and lashing of equipment and stores into gliders was usually the responsibility of the ancillary units themselves.) Some of the first parachutists to qualify at Ringway were RASC personnel: a divisional supply column was divided into air and ground teams; the former being responsible for loading and ejecting pre-allocated stores from the aircraft and the latter for jumping with the division and sorting out the stores on the ground. The probable isolation of airborne troops during a prolonged period of envelopment postulated a large base organisation capable of administering reserve supplies at home airfields and mounting frequent air re-supply sorties. Two main supply groups were in operation in 1944, one in the United Kingdom and one in the Far East. The primary units of these supply groups were the air despatch companies flown by Allied aircrew on airborne operations and on regular supply missions to partisan groups.

In 1944 the air despatch companies handled three types of containers: the wicker pannier, the bombcell container and the SEAC pack. The pannier carried a load of 500 lbs and was pushed into and despatched from the door of the aircraft by means of a roller conveyer. The hinged, two-compartment, metal bombcells, which were just long enough to take .303 Lee Enfield rifles or Bren light machine-guns, could be slung on the underside of wings and fuselage of any aircraft fitted with universal bomb racks. Small, fast fighter bombers loaded with three or four bombcells were especially useful on supply missions for dodging the fire of anti-aircraft guns. The SEAC pack was introduced in the Far East and many thousands were dropped in the jungles of Burma; these canvas containers held 200 lbs, and it was important to pack them to the maximum weight to prevent drifting.

On supply missions of every kind pilots took their aircraft down to a dropping level of 600 feet or below depending on the type of parachute in use and even hedge-hopped at fifty feet to free-drop non-breakable items such as rubber tyres. Canopies were made in various sizes and from different materials but the types adopted for the European theatre were mostly the 24-ft and 28-ft varieties made of cotton, nylon or silk. Two kinds of 18-ft 'chute manufactured specially for air supply were used in the Far East where the jute hessian produced in India was a cheap but effective choice of material for supply parachutes.

As Spring 1944 receded and warmer days in Britain were prescient for many of a bloody summer, Lieutenant-General Browning on 24th April mounted a British 1st Airborne Corps exercise that ranged for three days over the green fields of Oxfordshire, Wiltshire and Gloucestershire. Exercise 'Mush' in which 6th Airborne was lifted by air and 1st Airborne acted as the enemy on the ground was the dress rehearsal for 6th Airborne's share in the invasion of North West Europe. No 38 Group since January operating with No 46 Group (Dakotas) under Air Vice-Marshal Hollinghurst and in liaison with the United States 9th Troop Carrier Command were now based on twenty-two airfields in Southern England and in East Anglia.

On 8th May the Supreme Commander Allied Forces Europe, General Dwight D. Eisenhower, designated D-Day as 5th June, but because of the bad weather he decided to postpone the assault on the Normandy coastline until the following day. 2,876,000 men were ready to cross the English Channel for the greatest seaborne military operation in history; over 20,000 invasion troops being scheduled to go ashore from ships and craft on D-Day, plus 1 and 2. Commencing at 06.30 hours on 6th June the

United States First Army was due to land on the right of the line on the Cotentin Peninsula south-east of Cherbourg on Utah and further east on Omaha beaches, and the British Second Army including the Canadian 3rd Division fifty minutes later on the left on Gold, Juno and Sword beaches. Some 5,000 vessels made up the cross-Channel fleet and RAF bombers were poised to strike along the entire invasion coast.

The American attack was to be spearheaded by the US 82nd and 101st Airborne Divisions landing from the air shortly after midnight astride the Merderet River in the vicinity of St-Mère Eglise to facilitate the advance of the US 7th Corps. At the same time the British 6th Airborne Division landing forty miles to the east was to secure the Allied left flank between the Orne and Dives rivers. 3rd and 5th Parachute Brigades dropping in the early hours of D-Day on the high ground north-east of Caen together with 6th (Air-Landing) Brigade mostly arriving the following afternoon were to consolidate in the area and both capture and destroy road and railway bridges over the Caen Canal, Orne and Dives rivers. The original plan to withdraw the division from Normandy immediately after the link-up on the first day was altered by 'Monty' himself: he wanted the airborne not only to secure but to hold and defend 21st Army Group's exposed left flank; an assignment honourably fulfilled by the 'red berets' for a period of thirteen weeks in the line.

On 20th June General Eisenhower approved the organisation of the First Allied Airborne Army. This army was to comprise the British 1st Airborne Corps, consisting of 1st and 6th Airborne Divisions, 1st Special Air Service Brigade and 1st Polish Independent Parachute Brigade Group; the US 18th Airborne Corps, made up of the 17th, 82nd and 101st Airborne Divisions (and later the 13th) and several Airborne Aviation Battalions; the British 52nd (Lowland) Division re-assigned from a mountain rôle to fly in transport planes; 9th US Troop Carrier Command, and Nos 38 and 46 Groups RAF. Lieutenant-General Lewis H. Brereton was selected to lead the new Airborne army with Browning as British Corps Commander and Deputy Army Commander. (This incidentally was the same Brereton who in autumn 1918 was delegated by Billy Mitchell to plan the Metz parachute operation.) The US 18th Corps was commanded by Matthew B. Ridgway, who had led the 82nd 'All American' Division from North Africa into Sicily, Italy and Normandy.

At the beginning of September Field Marshal Montgomery, whose onward drive into Belgium had stalled, proposed regaining the advance with a powerful thrust into Holland and across the Rhine into Germany. General Dempsey's British Second Army with Horrocks' XXX Corps in the centre was then positioned on the line of the Albert Canal with a bridgehead over the Meuse Escaut Canal. In this bridgehead the Guards Armoured Division stood astride the main highway leading northwards from the Dutch frontier through Eindhoven, Nijmegen, Arnhem and Apeldoorn to the Zuider Zee. The road to Arnhem on the Lower Rhine offered a means of creating a corridor through the enemy defences into Germany. The West Wall that protected the German homeland lay less than forty miles to the east and ended at Goch a few miles south of the Reichswald Forest. Montgomery's idea was to turn the flank of the frontier defences by advancing across the Lower Rhine at Arnhem and to then wheel eastwards into the North German Plain. All depended on the swift passage of armour along the sixty-mile stretch of highway from the Dutch frontier to Arnhem. But before this manoeuvre could be accomplished the Germans must first be prevented from destroying the intervening canal and river bridges.

In the event Montgomery's proposal for an almighty Allied offensive mounted by all available resources was considerably modified by Eisenhower. The main drive would come from Horrocks' XXX Corps, with VIII and XII Corps on its flanks. Three airborne divisions – the British 1st and US 82nd and 101st – forming the 1st Allied Airborne Corps were assigned to capture the bridges over the lateral water obstacles and secure the line of advance of Dempsey's Second Army. The US 101st Airborne Division (Taylor) was ordered to drop north of Eindhoven to capture the bridge over the Wilhelmina Canal at Zon and another bridge further north over the Zuid Willems Canal at Veghel. The US 82nd Airborne Division (Gavin) was to land south of Nijmegen on both sides of the highway near Grave. In this locality Jim Gavin's objectives were the bridge over the Maas River at Grave; the road and rail bridges over the Waal River at Nijmegen, and the Maas-Waal Canal bridge on the southern approach to Nijmegen. Furthest away Urquhart's British 1st Airborne Division with Sosabowski's Polish Parachute Brigade under command was to seize the road bridge at Arnhem. 52nd (Lowland) Division was scheduled to fly into Deelen airfield after consolidation in the Arnhem area. Lieutenant-General Browning whose headquarters was to be located in the neighbourhood of Nijmegen was chosen to command 1st Allied Airborne Corps.

After the invasion of France 1st Airborne Division was briefed for impending operations on D-Day plus 5, but the drop was cancelled and so were the next sixteen plans muted during the Normandy deadlock and after the break-out in July of 21st Army Group on the eastern sector across the Seine into Belgium. On 10th September Major-General Urquhart received his orders to capture the Arnhem 'bridges or a bridge' and establish a bridgehead to allow XXX Corps to deploy north of the Lower Rhine. The total number of officers and men of the division to be airborne numbered 10,095 including 1,126 glider pilots. Operation 'Market-Garden', the code name for the combined land/airborne offensive, was finally scheduled for Sunday 17th September.

3. Insignia, Clothing, Weapons, Equipment and Air Transport

1   2   3

Insignia and Clothing

In the early days airborne soldiers wore the hat badges and uniform insignia of their parent units. The Army Air Corps hat badge appeared shortly after the formation of the Army Air Corps and Glider Pilot Regiment in December 1941. Members of the Glider Pilot Regiment later wore their own distinctive hat badge. The emblem depicting Bellerophon astride the winged horse Pegasus was designed in light blue on a maroon square by Major Edward Seago. It was introduced in May 1942 and worn on both arms of all airborne soldiers. No special badges or signs existed to distinguish between 1st and 6th Airborne Divisions. The maroon beret chosen by General Browning was first worn by members of 1st Parachute Brigade in November 1942. The Parachute Regiment formed in August 1942 wore the AAC hat badge until it was replaced by its own winged parachute badge with crown and lion in May 1943. Support, service and air-landed infantry also wore the maroon beret but with their own hat badges.

The first parachute infantry units adopted the PARACHUTE shoulder titles in light blue on maroon, also with the '1', '2', '3' battalion figures incorporated below. Other airborne troops at this time wore AIRBORNE shoulder titles in the same colour scheme but more usually wore their parent unit titles. The rectangular AIRBORNE flash was always worn below the Pegasus arm flash. When the Parachute Regiment came into being, it adopted the shoulder title PARACHUTE REGIMENT in dark blue lettering on a light blue background. The shoulder titles borne by the Glider Pilot

1) Canvas foam rubber helmet. 2) Rimmed steel helmet. 3) Rimless steel helmet with camouflage netting.

Regiment also appeared in dark blue on a light blue background and read GLIDER PILOT REGT. The Pathfinders of the 21st and 22nd Independent Parachute Companies displayed the numerals XXI and XXII below their respective shoulder titles. 1st Canadian Parachute Battalion (6th Airborne Division) wore their own winged parachute hat badge and shoulder titles but with Pegasus and AIRBORNE arm flashes.

Special lanyards were worn by five of the parachute battalions: green (1st), yellow (2nd), red (3rd), black (4th), light blue (12th). The 4th (Wessex) Battalion also painted its webbing black. The 5th (Scottish) Battalion drawn from the Camerons wore the Balmoral bonnet with the AAC badge on a Hunting Stewart tartan, and the AIRBORNE shoulder title until September 1944. The 6th Battalion wore the Royal Welch back flash at the back of the collar.

Qualified parachutists at first received miniature parachute wings worn above the left breast pocket. The definitive wings badge was the white parachute with light blue wings on a khaki backing. This cloth badge, which was awarded for completing seven jumps, was sewn below the right shoulder title. These wings if sewn above the left breast pocket of a Service tunic denoted an SOE operator and were awarded to the man or woman concerned on returning to the UK after an operational jump. A para-

56

Selected Wings,Shoulder Titles and Arm Flashes

chute emblem worn on the left forearm meant that the wearer was a qualified parachutist but did not serve in an airborne unit. Glider pilots wore their wings on the left breast: 1st Glider Pilots, gold crown and lion with light blue wings on a dark blue backing; 2nd Glider Pilots, gold 'G' and circle instead of the crown and lion. Glider infantry wore a small glider insignia on the left forearm. The 1st Canadian Parachute Battalion favoured a large winged parachute emblem worn on the left breast. RAF parachute jumping instructors were eventually allowed to wear a white parachute with laurel leaves on the right upper arm.

British airborne troops wore the maroon beret, standard khaki serge battledress, with web waist belt, web gaiters and ammunition boots. Officers were also issued with the usual service dress and the Parachute Regiment in common with other units adopted collar badges. Overseas dress was appropriate to the theatre.

After the early experiments in combat clothing, the Denison smock became standard airborne issue. This garment was windproof but only semi-waterproof. It was unlined and not especially warm but this was an advantage under active combat conditions. Four external patch pockets fastened by press studs were provided as well as two internal pockets. The camouflage pattern was ragged with brown and dark green patches printed over a light green base. A tail piece was sewn to the rear hem of the smock and was usually fastened back with press studs. The flap was in the habit of falling loose: much to the amusement of the Arabs in North Africa; their name for the paratroopers being 'the men with donkey tails'. The Denison smock was worn over the BD blouse, or over a shirt or shirt and pullover.

The earliest form of protective headgear worn by a paratrooper was the black, leather flying helmet. At least four versions of the cloth-covered sorbo rubber helmet were developed for training purposes but there was no substitute for a steel helmet in action. The rounded airborne steel helmet with chin strap worn at the time of the Bruneval raid displayed a curved rim. The rim was gradually eliminated in later models; the final rimless version with chin strap being similar to the crown of a bowler hat.

The airborne soldier's basic webbing equipment consisted of the standard issue small pack, which was supported by two shoulder straps, and two ammunition pouches fixed to the belt and secured to the body by two narrow, supporting straps. The small pack contained such items as mess tins, knife, fork, spoon, medical pack, washing and cleaning gear, spare shirt, socks and other miscellaneous items for personal maintenance. (No special lightweight rations were issued, the troops receiving normal compo. issue tins in boxes.) Additional items of equipment carried on the belt or around the body were the water bottle and carrier, bayonet and frog, entrenching tool with haft and carrier and a toggle rope. Officers and some NCOs carried a prismatic compass and binoculars. A piece of camouflage netting described as a face veil was invariably worn as a scarf.

Weapons

Divisional allocation:

Sub-machine-guns	6,504	75-mm Pack How	18
Rifles	7,171	Light AA	23
Pistols	2,942	2-in mortars	474
LMGs (Bren)	966	3-in mortars	56
MMGs (Vickers)	46	4.2-in mortars	5
PIATs	392	Flame-throwers	38
6-pdr Atk	84	Tanks (light)	11
17-pdr Atk	16	Tanks (overland)	11

Sub-machine-guns

Thompson gun. The Thompson was in general service in the British Army in 1940–41 but was largely replaced by the Sten gun. The 'Tommy gun' remained popular with the Commandos and other special raiding units throughout the war. Auto-Ordnance Corp., USA, held the Thompson patent but manufacture was delegated under licence. Of .45-in calibre, the A1, which was operated on the principle of delayed blowback, was fitted alternatively for 50-round drum or 20-/30- round box magazines. Method of fire was selective, muzzle velocity 920 feet per second and the maximum rate was estimated at 600–725 rounds per minute. The A1 displayed twin hand grips with finger notches; it weighed about 11 lbs and was 33.7 inches in length. In 1941 the new M1 based on the Thompson design dispensed with the drum magazine. The 'Tommy gun' was a clumsy weapon but reasonably accurate up to 50 yards or more.

Left.
A sergeant poses with a Thompson sub-machine-gun at Ringway before a practice jump. He is carrying a respirator across his chest.

Right.
Sten machine carbine

Sten gun. The Sten machine carbine was produced as a cheap expedient after the Dunkirk disaster. Designed and developed by R. V. Shepperd and H. J. Turpin at the Royal Small Arms Factory at Enfield, the name 'Sten' derived from the initial letters of the inventors' surnames and the first two letters of the place of origin. Altogether five versions were produced starting with the Mk I in June 1941. The calibre 9-mm Sten was made of sheet metal tubing; a 32-round box magazine was slotted into a receiver on the left side of the barrel. The version produced in greatest quantity was the Mk II with its single tube shoulder stock. Method of fire was selective, muzzle velocity 1,425 feet per second and the maximum rate was 500 rounds per minute. The single feed system was a frequent cause of jamming. The Mk II weighed nearly 7 lbs and was 30 inches in length. Mks I, III and IV displayed triangular tube stocks but the Mk V, which was fitted with a bayonet, was equipped with a more solid wooden butt. The Sten gun proved effective up to 100 yards.

Rifles

Lee Enfield Rifle. In 1939 the standard rifle in the British Army was the Short Magazine Lee Enfield (SMLE) dating from 1902. The SMLE was in theory gradually replaced by the Rifle No 4 Mk I. The .303 calibre Lee Enfield was a magazine-fed, bolt action shoulder rifle. The detachable magazine contained 10 rounds; rate of fire was 5 single shots per minute (normal), 15 single shots per minute (rapid); the muzzle velocity of the weapon being 2,440 feet per second. The No 4 Mk I weighing 8.75 lbs was 44.5 inches in length. Front sights were of the blade variety and the rear sights vertical leaf with either aperture battle sights or the 'L' type. The sighting was flexible up to an effective range of 600 yards. The Mk II was very similar to the Mk I. The Rifle No 5 Mk I at 7.15 lbs in weight and 39.5 inches in length was lighter and shorter than the No 4 rifle. The bayonet for all marks was a short spike. Another version of the No 4 rifle was the No 4 (T) equipped with telescopic sights for snipers.

Pistols

Webley, Smith and Wesson revolvers and the Colt Browning automatic pistol. The standard side arm of the British Army from 1936 until 1957 was the Webley (Enfield) .38-in Revolver No 2 Mk 1. The method of operation was based on single or double action. The weight of the revolver was 1 lb 11½ ounces and the length 10.25 inches (barrel 5 inches); the cylinder discharged 6 ball cartridges from separate chambers; the muzzle velocity of the weapon being 600 feet per second. The effective range was 'point blank', ie 20 yards, and a steady grip was mandatory.

Large quantities of the US .38-inch Smith and Wesson revolvers and British Webley .45 were also carried by British soldiers. Both discharged 6 rounds. A magazine-fed .45 SL Webley pistol fired 7 rounds.

The Colt .45 automatic pistol was issued to airborne and Commando units only but as the 9-mm Browning superseded the Webley revolver as the official side arm in the post-war years. The US .45-inch Model A1 automatic pistol made by Colt and adopted by the US Army in 1926 was evolved from the previous Colt model of 1911, which in fact was originated by Browning in 1897. The weight of the pistol was 2.43 lbs and the length 8.62 inches (barrel 5 inches); the magazine contained 7 rounds; the muzzle velocity being 810 feet per second. The Colt automatic was effective at 50 yards. The Colt .45 was adapted for 9-mm ammunition; the Browning magazine containing 13 rounds held in double row.

Machine-guns

Bren Light Machine-Gun. This weapon had its origin in the Czech ZB 30,

which was adapted to British requirements in the 1930s to fire .303 rimmed rounds. The name 'Bren' was made up from the first two letters of Brno, the town of origin, and Enfield, the town of manufacture. A Bren was supported on the ground by adjustable bipod or tripod pivots and was also fired from the hip. The armoured Bren carrier, a tracked vehicle, gave the gunner protection and manoeuvrability. Two Brens mounted together formed a useful anti-aircraft weapon. Air-cooled, gas-operated, the Mk I was fed with .303 ball cartridges from either 30-round curved box or 100-round drum magazines. The trigger mechanism provided for three positions: safety, automatic and single shots. The rate of fire was 60 rounds per minute (normal), 120 rounds per minute (rapid), the muzzle velocity being 2,440 feet per second. Maximum rate of fire was 450–550 rounds per minute. A barrel when overheated was substituted by a spare barrel. The Mk I weighing 23 lbs was 4.5 inches in length (barrel 25 inches). Front sights were of the blade type with ears and the rear sights the aperture type with radial drum. Effective range on a bipod was 500 yards, maximum 2,000 yards. Production was simplified with the introduction of the Mk II model. The Bren LMG is still in service, its barrel standardised to NATO 7.62-mm specification.

Vickers Medium Machine-Gun. This was Britain's basic infantry machine-gun in both world wars. The British Vickers differed little from its predecessor, the Maxim, and was introduced in 1912 as the Vickers Maxim. Water-cooled, belt-fed, the Mk I was recoil operated, with gas boost from the muzzle booster. The barrel was cooled by $7\frac{1}{2}$ pints of water; the canvas belt contained 250 .303 ball cartridges. Maximum rate of fire was 450 to 550 rounds per minute and the muzzle velocity 2,440 feet per second. The Mk I weighing 90 lbs all up (ie gun and tripod) was 43 inches in length (barrel 28.4 inches). Two men were needed to load and fire the gun; an extra man being useful to help carry the gun, tripod and ammunition and water containers. The Vickers MMG was rugged, reliable and effective at 2,000 yards. The Mk I model was officially listed as the airborne medium machine-gun, 1940–45.

Anti-tank weapons

PIAT. The Projector Infantry Anti-tank Mk I was introduced in 1940 as a replacement for the Boys' anti-tank rifle. The PIAT, which was similar to the American bazooka, was designed to project a hollow-charge grenade. The 3-lb grenade was supported for the first part of its flight on a central spigot. In the projector the grenade's recoil forces re-cocked the firing mechanism. The PIAT weighing 32 lbs was 39 inches in length; the muzzle velocity being 240–450 feet per second. Effective range was 100 yards.

Grenades. The two that featured most prominently in the anti-tank rôle were the Hand Grenade, No 74 (ST), and the Hawkins Grenade, No 75. No 74 (ST), the 'Sticky Bomb', was covered in an adhesive coating to enable it to stick to the side of a tank. (More often than not it stuck to the thrower.) It weighed 36 ounces and operated on a 5-second time fuze. No 75 (Hawkins), which used a crush igniter, could be thrown as a grenade or placed in the ground as a mine. Clusters were used against the heavier tanks. It measured 40 cubic inches and weighed 36 ounces, half of which was made of a bursting charge.

Gammon bomb (No 82 Grenade). A plastic explosive charge developed from the 'Sticky Bomb' and designed by Captain R. J. Gammon MC of 1st Parachute Battalion. The explosive was placed in a stockinet bag which contained a detonator mechanism in a screw cap at the neck. It was also used for demolitions and as an anti-personnel grenade.

6-pounder gun. This weapon was designed in Britain in 1938 but not issued until September 1941. It was replaced in the Royal Artillery in 1943 by the 17-pounder but continued to serve as an infantry support weapon on all fronts. The calibre of the 6-pounder Mk II was 2.244 inches, the length of the barrel 100 inches and the all-up weight approximately one ton. The rate of fire was 10 rounds per minute; the muzzle velocity being 2,700 feet per

The shield will be removed from the 6-pounder gun before it follows the jeep up the ramp of the Horsa glider.

second. Effective armour-penetrating range was 1,000 yards but the 6-pounder could not cope with the frontal armour of the German Tiger Tank. The Mks II and IV were the towed anti-tank guns.

Artillery

75-mm Pack Howitzer. Designed in the USA as a mountain weapon suitable for mule transport, the 75-mm was the primary artillery support weapon of an airborne division. This low velocity howitzer was typical of the weapons that needed hollow charge or squashhead shells to give them a chance against tanks. The length of the barrel was 52 inches and the all-up weight approximately half a ton. The initial rate of fire was 6 rounds per minute; the muzzle velocity with high explosive shell being 1,250 feet per second. The effective range was 9,475 yards.

Anti-aircraft weapons. The universal 40-mm Bofors, used by almost every combatant during the Second World War, was adapted for use as a light-weight AA weapon. The Bofors fired a 2-lb shell at the rate of 120 rounds per minute. The barrel could be removed for stowing on board a glider. The 20-mm Hispano Suiza (Oerlikon) was also employed for air defence.

Mortars

OML 2-in Mortar. Muzzle-loaded, the 2-in mortar was an invaluable weapon in the support rôle. Developed in the 1930s, the weapon was issued in large numbers to infantry battalions. Quick into action, it fired 2¼-lb HE or 2-lb smoke bombs with great accuracy over a range of 500 yards. Elevation was alternatively high or low angle and the maximum rate of fire was 8 rounds per minute. The overall length of the weapon was 21 inches. The weapon weighed 19 lbs with base or 10⅛ lbs with spade and the HE bomb 2 lbs 4 ounces. The 2-in mortar also fired illuminating and signal ammunition. Mks VII and VIII were assigned as the airborne models.

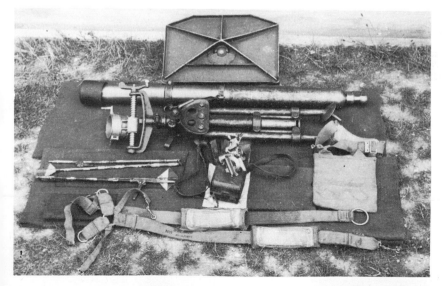

3-inch mortar stripped down less base plate for packing in an equipment container.

OML 3-in Mortar. This was the standard medium mortar issued to the battalion heavy weapon companies. Developed from the Stokes mortar of the First World War, the 3-in mortar was muzzle-loaded and fired 10-lb HE, smoke and illuminating bombs. The overall length of the weapon was 51 inches. The mortar weighed 42 lbs, the mounting 45 lbs, and the base plate 37 lbs. Minimum elevation was 45 degrees and the maximum 80 degrees. The maximum effective range was 1,600 yards and the rate of fire 5 rounds per minute.

OML 4.2-in Mortar. The weight of the 4.2-in mortar was 257 lbs. Its maximum effective range was 4,100 yards.

Equipment

Many ingenious items of equipment were designed or adapted for airborne forces but these mainly referred to the needs of the support and service units. (The inventory is too numerous to list.) The basic transport allocation included only one innovation, namely the lightweight, collapsible Corgi motor-cycle, which was to have some considerable influence on post-war methods of travel. The following transport items were not all necessarily lifted by air on specific operations.

Divisional transport allocation:

Trade bicycles	1,907	Trailers	935
Folding bicycles	1,362	Handcarts	450
Heavy motor-cycles	704	Carriers	25
Lightweight motor-cycles	529	Scout cars	25
15-cwt trucks	129	Miscellaneous vehicles	115
Jeeps	904		

The Wellbike 2-stroke motor-cycle conveniently fitted into an equipment container. Specially invented for paratroopers, the Wellbike measured 4 ft 3 ins long × 15 ins broad. The handle bars, steering column and saddle were arranged on a collapsible principle. The maximum speed of the machine was 30 mph and the maximum range was 90 miles on one filling of 6½ pints of petrol. The weight (less petrol) was 70 lbs.

Equipment containers, open and closed for dropping. 1) contains an 18 (wireless) set, 2) contains a 21 (wireless) set, 3) shows both containers closed for dropping. 4) Two bombcell containers; .303 rifle and Bren gun on the right. 5) Loading a bombcell equipment container for dropping. A pilot 'chute operated by static-line released the main 'chute. Canopies came in different colours for company and battalion DZ identification.

Loading a jeep into a Horsa glider. On operations a Cordtex explosive ring was fitted to blow the fuselage apart if necessary on landing.

Parachute Type 'X' Equipment

The 'X'-type 'chute consisted of four parts:

The parachute had a flat canopy of bias construction and measured 28 feet across when laid out on the ground. A circular vent in the centre measured 22 inches in diameter. All the earlier types of canopy were made of silk but later cotton parachutes known as 'Ramex' were introduced as an alternative to silk. These canopies differed in that the 'D' panels adjoining the vent were made of a porous and stronger cloth than the remainder of the canopy. Nylon canopies were manufactured towards the end of the war.

28 rigging lines each 25 feet long and with a minimum breaking strength of 400 lbs were brought together below the periphery in four groups each of 7 lines, each group terminating in a 'D' ring. Each rigging line passed continuously from one 'D' ring over the canopy and vent and down a second 'D' ring on the other side. The lines were made of silk or nylon.

The inner bag (Mk I) consisted of a bag of rectangular section with an open end which could be closed by two small triangular flaps. A large flap formed an extension of the back of the bag and was used for stowing the rigging lines. The stowages were either elastic cords or webbing loops. When the canopy was packed in the bag the mouth was closed by a tie which passed through the beckets on the triangular flaps and on the top and bottom edges of the mouth of the bag and was held there by two weak ties. The Mk II bag had the rigging lines stowed in webbing loops on the front of the bag.

The outer pack. Both versions (Mks I and II) were similar in design and closely resembled an envelope, the four flaps being at the front. In the Mk I design the static-line was stowed in two pockets outside the pack, and paid out from a point where the four flaps met. In the Mk II design the static-line was stowed inside the pack and paid out from an opening at the top of the pack.

The harness. The man sat in a seat strap formed by the main suspension straps passing in a continuous line from one set of rigging lines under the man's seat and up the other set of lines. He was held in this position by shoulder, back, chest and leg straps. The metal strap attachments clipped into a metal box which was permanently fastened to one of the chest straps. The man was locked into his harness by giving the circular metal disc controlling the box device a $\frac{1}{4}$-turn in a clockwise direction. The parts of the harness between the shoulders and the rigging lines were called lift webs. The lift webs divided above the shoulders and a measure of flight control could be achieved by pulling down on one or two of the lift webs. One single thickness of webbing supported a minimum breaking load of 3,000 lbs. All metal fittings were made of forged stainless steel.

Gliders

GAL Hotspur. The Hotspur was manufactured by General Aircraft Ltd of Feltham, Middlesex. The Mk I was intended as a troop transport and had a wing span of 61 ft 6 ins. The Mk II had wings of reduced span and was used as the operational trainer. The Mk III was the elementary trainer.

The main differences between the Mks II and III were that the former was
towed from the nose and had a braced tail. A mid-wing cantilever monoplane, the Hotspur was of wooden construction with plywood coverings.
The cockpit in the nose was fitted for dual control with the pilots sitting
in tandem. The Mk III had a complete duplication of controls for each
pilot. Access to the six-seat troop compartment was through a door on the
port side. (Ballast was often used instead of troops.)

Weight loaded (Mk III) 3,635 lbs.
Span 45 ft $10\frac{3}{4}$ ins, Length 39 ft $8\frac{3}{4}$ ins, Height 10 ft 10 ins, Wing area
272 sq ft.
Maximum towing speed 150 mph, Maximum diving speed 170 mph,
Stalling speed 54 mph.

Airspeed Horsa. The Horsa Mk I, a troop and freight carrying glider, was
manufactured by Airspeed Ltd of Portsmouth, Hampshire. The Airspeed Horsa was a high-wing cantilever monoplane. Both wings and fuselage were all-wooden constructions with plywood coverings; the wooden

Hotspur glider.

Below
Horsa glider.

tail being covered in fabric. The pilots – operating dual control – sat side-by-side in a cabin in the extreme nose of the glider. Two large fuselage doors were situated port side forward for freight and starboard side aft for troops. As a trooper, the Horsa contained 25 seats but normally carried only 15 fully armed troops. A wide variety of military equipment could alternatively be stowed in the main compartment.

The Mk II introduced in 1944 was of the same length and wing span as the Mk I. The Mk II, however, displayed a hinged nose to permit the direct loading and unloading of light ordnance and vehicles..The Horsa flew under both British and American colours on the Normandy invasion.

Weight loaded (Mk I) 15,500 lbs, Wing loading 14.05 lbs/sq ft.
Span 88 ft, Length 67 ft, Height 19 ft 6 ins, Wing area 1,104 sq ft.
Maximum towing speed 160 mph, Maximum diving speed 180 mph., Stalling speed 60 mph.

GAL Hamilcar. The Hamilcar was designed by General Aircraft Ltd of Feltham, Middlesex, and produced by the Birmingham Railway Carriage and Wagon Co Ltd. This heavy-duty glider was originally designed to carry the Tetrarch tank or 2 Bren-carriers. Later, however, it was adapted for the carriage of a great variety of military loads. It was towed by Halifax, Lancaster or Stirling 4-engined bombers. A high-wing cantilever monoplane, the Hamilcar was made of wood and metal. The flight compartment was in the upper portion of the forward fuselage seating two in tandem with dual controls. Access to this compartment was by ladder on the inner starboard side of the fuselage, through a hatch in the roof and along the top of the centre-section. The nose of the fuselage was hinged to starboard for loading. Adjustable vehicle rails were fitted to the floor of the fuselage.

Weight loaded 36,000 lbs (Wing loading 22.37 lbs/sq ft).
Span 110 ft, Length 68 ft, Height (tail down) 20 ft 3 ins, Wing area 1,657.5 sq ft.
Maximum towing speed 150 mph, Maximum diving speed 187 mph, Stalling speed 65 mph.

Waco CG-4A (British name: Hadrian). British troops flew as passengers in the American Waco glider on the Sicily invasion and on Chindit operations in Burma. This glider was designed by the Waco Aircraft Co, Troy, Ohio, and was manufactured in fifteen factories in different parts of the United States. The CG-4A was a rigidly-braced high-wing monoplane of fabric-covered wood and steel-tube construction. It could carry freight or 15 fully-armed troops, two of whom were the pilot and co-pilot. 2 pilots sat side by side with dual controls in the nose of the glider. The nose was hinged for direct loading of equipment. The normal troop entrance was port side forward. The CG-4A could also be fitted with 2 'power eggs', ie 2 cells each containing a 6-cylinder engine, fuel tank and engine instruments.

Weight loaded 7,500 lbs, Wing loading 8.81 lbs/sq ft.
Span 83 ft 8 ins, Length 48 ft 3¾ ins, Height 12 ft 8 ins, Wing area 851 sq ft.
Maximum towing speed 125 mph, Minimum gliding speed 38 mph.

Hamilcar glider and Tetrarch tank.

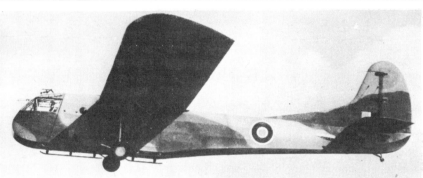

Waco CG-4A (Hadrian) glider on tow.

Glider tugs and carrier aircraft

Armstrong Whitworth Albemarle. Conceived by the Armstrong Whitworth Company of Coventry as a twin-engined bomber-reconnaissance aircraft, the Albemarle was widely used as a glider tug. The Albemarle also saw service as a paratroop aircraft; 10 men dropping through a large hole in the rear fuselage floor. A mid-wing cantilever monoplane, it was made almost exclusively of wood and steel. All marks (with the exception of Mark IV) were powered by two Bristol 'Hercules XI' 14-cylinder radial engines; weight empty as a glider tug and as a paratroop-carrier was 22,600 lbs. Maximum speed was over 250 mph and range 1,350 miles.

The Mk I (Series II), Mk S.T.I. (Series II), Mk II, Mk V and Mk VI (Series I and II) were all equipped as glider tugs. The Mk II, Mk V and Mk VI (Series I and II) were alternatively paratroop-carriers. The Mk S.T.I. (Series I) and the Mk VI (Series I and II) were special transports.

Span 77 ft, Length 59 ft 11 ins, Height 15 ft 7 ins, Wing area 803.5 sq ft.

Armstrong Whitworth Whitley. From the same stable as the Albemarle, the twin-engined Whitley was also originally a bomber-reconnaissance aircraft. The Whitley carried out the first paratroop operation over southern Italy in February 1941. It was withdrawn from production in 1942. The Mk V was converted as the paratroop aircraft. 10 men dropped through a hole in the floor of the fuselage. The Mk V also served as a glider tug. The power was provided by 2 Rolls-Royce 'Merlin X' 12-cylinder engines and the weight with full military load was 25,550 lbs. Maximum speed (Mk V) was 230 mph and the range 2,400 miles.

Span 84 ft, Length 72 ft 6 ins, Height 15 ft, Wing area 1,138 sq ft.

The Douglas C-47 'Skytrain' (British name: Dakota 1). The C-47 manufactured by the Douglas Aircraft Company Inc of Santa Monica, California, was a military adaptation of the DC-3 airliner. The C-47 was essentially a freight carrier and displayed a reinforced metal floor, a large loading door and reinforced landing gear. The twin-engined Dakota was a low-wing cantilever monoplane. In the supply rôle it carried up to 6,000 lbs of equipment, *eg* two jeeps or three crated aero engines with sufficient fuel for a range of 1,500 miles. As a paratroop aircraft, it was equipped with folding benches for twenty-eight fully-armed troops. Exits were performed from the door, which was located port side aft. The Dakota from mid-1942 was the workhorse of British and American parachute forces and served also as a glider tug. The power was provided by 2 Pratt and Whitney 'Twin Wasp' R-1830 engines and the weight with full military load was 26,000 lbs. (Wing loading 25.3 lbs/sq ft). Maximum speed was 229 mph and the range 1,500 miles.

Span 95 ft, Length 64 ft $5\frac{1}{2}$ ins, Height 16 ft $11\frac{1}{2}$ ins, Wing area 987 sq ft.

Handley Page Halifax. Manufactured by Handley Page Ltd of Cricklewood, London, the first production Halifax flew in October 1940. Principally a 4-engined heavy bomber, the Halifax was in continuous service until the end of the war. The aircraft was also allocated to glider squadrons and occasionally flew as a paratroop aircraft from some overseas stations. A mid-wing cantilever monoplane, 6 versions had appeared by early 1945; they differed significantly in specification. The Mk III, which saw service with airborne forces, was powered by 4 Bristol Hercules XVI radial engines and the weight loaded was 65,000 lbs (Wing loading 51 lbs/sq ft). The maximum speed was 270 mph and the range 3,000 miles.

Span 104 ft, Length 71 ft 7 ins, Height 20 ft 9 ins, Wing area 1,250 sq ft.

Short Stirling. Manufactured by Short Bros Ltd of Rochester, Kent, the Stirling preceded the Halifax as Britain's first 4-engined heavy bomber by a few months. By 1944, 5 versions had appeared and the aircraft was already obsolescent. The Stirling was then adapted as a transport, paratroop and tug aircraft but achieved its greatest success as a parachute supply aircraft. A mid-wing cantilever monoplane, the support aircraft were the Mks IV and V. A large opening in the underside of the rear fuselage of the Mk IV was introduced for the dropping of 24 paratroopers. Bombcells were retained and used for the carriage and dropping of airborne supplies. 34 air-landing troops could alternatively be carried

Armstrong
Whitworth
Albemarle, Mark V

Dakota C-47B
seen snapping up a
Waco CG-4A.

Handley Page
Halifax, Mark III.

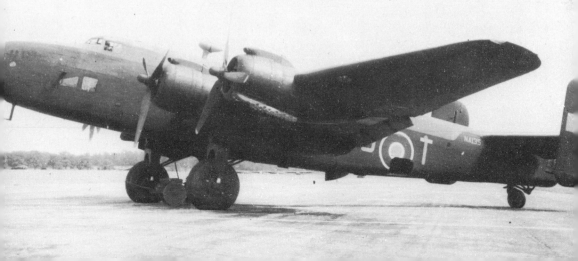

Stirling Mark IV.

The twin-engined Dakota C-47 was the workhorse of Allied airborne forces.

with arms and equipment. The Mk IV was also fitted for glider-towing. The Mk V was equipped for a variety of duties, including: (a) military passenger transport with 14 seats; (b) ambulance for 12 stretcher cases plus sitting cases; (c) troop transport for 40 fully-armed troops; (d) paratroop transport for 20 men and containers; (e) heavy freighter to carry one jeep, trailer and 6-pounder gun, or 2 jeeps with crew of 8 men, or 14 freight baskets, etc. Power was provided for the Mks IV and V by 4 Bristol Hercules XVI radial engines. Loaded weight in each case was 70,000 lbs (Wing and power loading 10.6 lbs/hp.) Maximum speed for Mks IV and V was 280 mph and the range 3,000 miles.

Span 99 ft 1 in, Length 87 ft 3 ins, Height 22 ft 9 ins, Wing area 1,460 sq ft.

4. Military Operations – The Red Devils

Operation 'Colossus'

At dawn on 9th February 1941 the eight Whitleys bearing Major T. A. G. Pritchard's 'X' Troop No 11 SAS Battalion flew into Malta on the completion of their 1,400 mile journey from Mildenhall in Suffolk. Final preparations for Operation 'Colossus', the Tragino Aqueduct Raid, were immediately set in motion: the following day six of the aircraft were loaded with arms containers packed with explosives, weapons, ammunition and rations and the other two aircraft fitted with bombs for a diversionary attack on railway marshalling yards at Foggia. The full party of thirty-eight parachutists allocated to the six carrier aircraft included three Italian interpreters, Private Nastri of the Rifle Brigade, Squadron Leader Lucky of the Royal Air Force and a 'Special' named Picchi. At 17.00 hours on the 10th the weather forecast was most encouraging and an hour later the eight Whitleys belonging to 91 Squadron RAF and led by Wing Commander J. B. Tait DFC were flying at 10,000 feet over Mount Etna bound for the Italian coast south of Salerno.

The five officers under Pritchard, apart from Lucky, were Captain C. G. Lea, Lieutenant A. J. Deane-Drummond and 2nd Lieutenant A. G. Jowett leading the covering parties and Captain G. F. K. Daly and 2nd Lieutenant G. R. Patterson (like Jowett, a Canadian), who were in charge of the sappers responsible for placing the explosives in position at the target. The drop was to be made on the north side of the aqueduct and after the mission was completed the men were to make their way on foot in small groups a distance of fifty miles to the west coast. His Majesty's Submarine *Triumph* was under orders to rendezvous with the parachute commandos on the night of 15th–16th February for the evacuation at the mouth of the River Sele.

Five of the Whitleys arrived bang on target and the drop commenced at about 21.45 hours: the small town of Calitri close to the Ofanto River and the Tragino aqueduct beyond were clearly visible in the bright moonlight to the parachutists on the run-in; but the pilot of the sixth Whitley with Captain Daly and his stick on board spent forty-five minutes circling the area before dropping the men in the next valley. The first soldier to land was Deane-Drummond, who came to earth in a ploughed field on the side of a hill overlooking the aqueduct. His section's objectives were to destroy a small bridge over the Genestra, a tributary of the Tragino stream, to hinder the possible arrival of the *carabinieri* and to concentrate all the peasants rounded up in the area in a cluster of nearby cottages. Lea and Jowett in charge of the other covering parties were stationed on either side of the Genestra bridge to observe movements up the valley. The fate of Daly and his engineer section was not then known to the others and Pritchard accordingly instructed the other RE officer, Patterson, to collect all the available sappers and get to work on the aqueduct. The intention was to blow all three piers but the loss of Daly's containers and two more that failed to leave their aircraft left the raiders short of explosives.

The central pier of the aqueduct was much taller than the outside pair, both resting more solidly, however, on rising ground on either side of the stream. The vulnerable parts of the structure were more accessible at the tops of the shorter piers and it was decided to place 800 lbs of gun cotton at one end only. A small supply of explosives had been diverted to the Genestra bridge and charges fused for firing as soon as the main target went up. At thirty minutes after midnight Patterson and his sappers had completed their preparatory work and Pritchard let off a single slab of gun cotton to warn all the raiders to move off to an assembly area. At this juncture Deane-Drummond ordered the firing of the charges at the Genestra bridge, which collapsed immediately, but the damp, night air caused a thirty-second delay in the detonation of the charges at the aqueduct. When the explosion occurred the men were sheltering behind a small hill and could not see the extent of the damage. Almost immediately the sound of a cascading waterfall was heard. Half of the aqueduct had collapsed – 'X' Troop had beyond doubt accomplished their mission.

At 01.30 hours and less than eight hours after leaving the comparative comforts of Malta behind, the parachute commandos set off briskly in three separate parties along different escape paths to the coast. The explosions were fortunately heard by Captain Daly's stick approaching in the distance and they turned without much hesitation and made for the coast. The proposed line of march lay generally in a south-westerly direction following the course of the River Sele itself through mountainous terrain until the river flowed into a small, coastal plain east of Eboli.

As it happened 'X' Troop's bid to escape was fated from the start. A radio signal received at the Malta base from one of the Whitleys ordered to bomb Foggia reported engine trouble and the pilot's intention of making a forced landing at the mouth of the River Sele. The pilot's choice of this emergency landing spot was purely coincidental but fears that the pick-up would be compromised by police and troops searching for the aircrew led to the cancellation of the *Triumph's* sailing orders.

Major Pritchard's party, which included Lieutenant Deane-Drummond, Picchi and Nastri, made about four miles along a high ridge before stopping to sleep for a few hours in a small ravine. On awakening the troops brewed up and basked in the warm sun while observing the lie of the land for the remaining hours of daylight. At nightfall the troops set off for the Sele watershed and after covering twenty miles Pritchard chose another hiding place – this time, amongst trees on top of a small hill.

As the men stretched out on the ground they were startled to see that a peasant had approached unobserved. The lone figure was soon joined by armed police and peasant folk, women and children included. Pritchard had no heart to open fire and toss grenades in the company of women and children and he accordingly ordered his men to lay down their arms. The remainder of 'X' Troop were also captured. The parties led by Lea and Jowett were picked up at about the same time near the village of Teora but Daly with his engineer section evaded capture until the fifth day when they were caught fifteen miles from the coast.

Conveyed in triumph by their captors to the prison in Naples, 'X' Troop was subjected to interrogation and all but Picchi eventually escorted handcuffed and in chains under heavy guard by train to the prisoner-of-war camp at Sulmona. Advised by his comrades to pose as a Free French soldier, Picchi refused and adamantly pressed home his political beliefs; two months later he was shot by a Fascist militia firing squad.

Operation 'Biting'

The temporary destruction of the Tragino aqueduct had no effect on the conduct of the war, but the RAF's success in dropping parachutists at night-time was an important factor in the selection of airborne troops for another Commando-style job. On 27th October 1941 the Lord Louis Mountbatten GCVO, DSO, ADC succeeded the venerable Sir Roger Keyes as Director of Combined Operations. Admiral Mountbatten also appreciated the potential of airborne forces and in January 1942 he discussed the Bruneval plan with Major-General Browning.

An effective German radar, the giant Würzburg, sent out medium length waves of sufficient accuracy to enable the flak gunners to engage unseen aircraft. Britain at that time possessed no comparable position finder or gun-layer radar and, as the Würzburg had been giving trouble to RAF flyers crossing the French Channel coast for over six months, British scientists were most anxious to study sample components of this superior radio-location equipment. Aerial photography clearly pinpointed one such station situated on a cliff-edge twelve miles north of Le Havre near the village of Bruneval.

Major John Frost.

The Bruneval raid planned for late February 1942 was to be a combined operation involving a company of parachute troops dropping from twelve Whitleys; a naval evacuation force, and an infantry party landed from the sea to cover the beach evacuation. 'C' Company, 2nd Parachute Battalion, was selected as the assault party and moved immediately from Ringway to commence training on the Salisbury Plain. The officer chosen to lead 'C' Company was Captain J. D. Frost, a Cameron, then undergoing his initial parachute training. The naval flotilla under Commander F. N. Cook, Royal Australian Navy, consisted of a small fleet of assault landing craft for the pick-up, support landing craft, motor gunboats and two escort destroyers. The beach protection party sailing in the support landing craft numbered thirty-two officers and men drawn from the Royal Fusiliers and South Wales Borderers. 51 Squadron RAF led by Wing Commander P. C. Pickard was detailed to supply the carrier aircraft; the RAF providing fighters for a diversionary raid at the time of the assault, and fighter cover for the withdrawal of the naval flotilla.

The radar apparatus was sited in front of a large, shabby-looking villa housing the technicians. About 400 yards along a track to the north a wood enclosed a farmhouse called La Presbytère. This farmhouse was the HQ of a small German garrison of about 100 troops who manned fifteen defence posts along the cliff. French intelligence sources providing this information also reported that an infantry regiment and a panzer battalion were stationed not far inland and could obviously send immediate reinforcements to the area. Apart from the wood, the ground stretching for several thousand yards behind the villa was completely flat and open and was ideally suited as a dropping zone. John Frost, who was now promoted to major, was at first under the impression that his assignment was to rehearse for a spectacular demonstration for VIP visitors; but when Flight Sergeant C. W. H. Cox, an expert radio engineer, arrived to join 'C' Company, Frost surmised that there was more to the job than met the eye. Cox, a quiet, unassuming man, had reported a few weeks previously to Ringway for 'a special mission'. Frost now learned from orders received from Major-General Browning that his company was to carry out a real raid on the coast of France; Cox had the key job of removing the radar components and bringing them back to England.

A final evacuation exercise was mounted on the night of Sunday, 23rd February, from a beach on Southampton Water. Favourable tide conditions at Bruneval at the projected time of withdrawal and a full moon dictated that the raid must take place within the next four nights. The weather forecasts over the next few days, however, were far from good but although on the 27th the French countryside was covered in snow, the wind had dropped and the visibility improved sufficiently to permit the drop that night. In the afternoon the naval flotilla put to sea and the airborne troops arrived in trucks at Thruxton airfield in Hampshire.

The operational plan called for 'C' Company to be divided into three groups, which were each code-named after prominent sailors. 'Nelson' group led by Lieutenant E. R. C. Charteris numbered forty men and was scheduled to drop first to knock out the machine-gun defences on the cliffs and move into Bruneval village. The largest group was called 'Drake' and consisted of fifty men sub-divided into two sections. Lieutenant P. A. Young's task was the seizure of the radar installation, which was built into a hole in the ground about 200 yards from the villa, and his party included Flight-Sergeant Cox, and Captain D. Vernon RE and his sappers, who were to help Cox take the apparatus to pieces. Major Frost's party would break into the villa and if possible take prisoners. 'Rodney' group comprising forty men under Lieutenant V. Timothy were ordered to prevent the Germans in La Presbytère from approaching the villa and to act as a reserve force. Bruneval itself is built on either side of a ravine leading down to the sea. The foot of the ravine some 1,200 yards from the villa was designated the company rendezvous area for the evacuation, which was timed for the naval craft coming in on the rising tide shortly after midnight.

The few who witnessed the Bruneval raiders clambering out of their transport vehicles at Thruxton to emplane in the waiting Whitleys, on 27th February 1942, must have been strangely moved by the sight of a company of paratroopers headed by pipers marching in faultless order around the airfield perimeter. The wild strains of the pipes have for centuries enthused a spirit of optimism and 'guid fecht' in the hearts of Scottish soldiers advancing into battle. The news about the fall of snow came too late for the men to obtain white camouflage clothing and it was now more than ever vital for them to act quickly on the ground. The flight of the twelve Whitleys to the French coast near Le Havre took two hours; the men huddled together in the cold, dark interiors of their aircraft sang to keep warm, played cards or tried to sleep. The expected landmarks illuminated by the bright moonlight were plainly visible through the open exit holes; but the coastal anti-aircraft batteries, helped also by the full moon, spotted the Whitleys and caused two of the pilots to alter course.

The DZ was located 1,000 yards east of the villa between two roads that converged on to a track leading to La Presbytère. All but the two stray Whitleys made the drop with complete accuracy; 100 men including Major Frost touching down in the right spot without serious injury. The very first move made by 'C' Company on French soil was to answer the call of nature; the steaming hot tea consumed in quantity at Thruxton having predictably reacted in flight. The suffering alleviated, 'C' Company less the two missing sections collected their gear from the containers and moved off to the assembly area. Lieutenant Charteris and half of the 'Nelson' group flying in the two Whitleys that took evasive action landed approximately 3,500 yards south of the villa – close to their second objective, the village, but a long way from their main objective, the machine-gun defences on the cliffs.

'Drake' and 'Rodney' groups advancing from the assembly area across the open ground proceeded in three parties to the radar installation, the villa and the wood surrounding La Presbytère. Lieutenant Young's party on discovering that the Würzburg radar, which looked incidentally like an enormous saucer, was actually manned at the time, immediately opened fire with sub-machine-guns, killing or capturing the crew. Major Frost threw a cordon around the villa and blowing his whistle led four men through the open door. As the men followed Frost up the stairs, they heard the burst of automatic fire coming from the direction of the radar and promptly killed a German soldier who was aiming shots at Young's party from an upstairs window. As the villa was otherwise empty Frost leaving two sentries withdrew his picquet to concentrate 'Drake' group around the radar set. Flight-Sergeant Cox and the sappers were already busy stripping down the apparatus and it was not long before Cox reported that he had removed all the component parts he needed.

The reaction expected from La Presbytère came when accurate fire was directed on 'Drake' group from the edge of the wood. Major Frost now ordered the withdrawal to the beach but not before one British soldier fell mortally wounded. Due to the non-arrival of 'Nelson' group in the target area, the machine-gun posts and pillboxes on the cliffs had not been touched and they were too numerous for Lieutenant Timothy's 'Rodney' group now also heading for the beach to tackle alone. Cox and his engineer section portering the radar equipment in the middle of the group were negotiating a difficult path through the snowdrifts. Lieutenant Charteris after forming up his two sections and finding his bearings had exchanged fire with a German foot patrol near Bruneval but made good time to meet Frost and the remainder of 'C' Company at the beach. Charteris and Timothy were at once ordered to take their men and clear all the machine-gun posts and pill boxes in line of sight of the beach.

At 02.15 hours the raiders were assembled on the beach waiting for the evacuation craft but none were in sight. Major Frost's signallers tried in

The Bruneval Raid, February 1942. The Navy brings men of 'C' Company, 2nd Parachute Battalion, safely into Portsmouth harbour. John Frost is on the bridge (second from left). The RAF officer standing in the centre of the group on the bridge is Nigel Norman.

vain to make contact on the air with the Navy and frantic attempts to communicate in the sea mist with an Aldiss lamp were also of no avail. The flotilla after avoiding a German destroyer had been lying off-shore for two hours when look-outs spotted signals from Very pistols exploding in the air above.the beach and three ALCs and three MTBs were rapidly despatched for the pick-up. The sight of the naval craft making a determined line through the mist for the beach came not a moment too soon. 'C' Company was now under heavy plunging fire from the cliff tops. Two men were dead and six had not reported to the RV but there was no time left to wait for them. The radar booty and six wounded men – amongst them Strachan, the company sergeant-major, who had three bullets in his stomach – were carefully put on board the ALCs. As the paratroopers embarked, the infantry leaping ashore from the MTBs contributed to the deafening noise with well-aimed fire at the cliff tops and were the last to leave the beach.

The troops were transferred on the open sea to the motor gunboats and the naval force headed for home. As the dawn broke a squadron of Spitfires swooped down from the sky to escort the flotilla to Portsmouth harbour. The Bruneval affair (Operation 'Biting') was declared a tremendous success; the radar equipment disclosed many secrets of German expertise and losses on the raid were slight.

Operation 'Freshman'

The scene now shifts to Telemark, the wild, mountainous region of Eastern Norway. As in many other areas of Norway, the falls at Rjukan have been harnessed to produce hydro-electric power on a tremendous scale. Before the war Norsk Hydro A/S at Rjukan was engaged in a side-line activity involving the production of deuterium oxide, or heavy water, which acts as a moderator in nuclear reaction. After the invasion of Norway in 1940 the Germans ordered Norsk Hydro to produce a substantial quantity of heavy water to assist them in their experiments to manufacture an atomic bomb. The existence of the heavy water plant situated actually at Vemork a few miles south-west of Rjukan was already known to the Allies but reports received in London about increased output at the plant were a matter of grave concern. Here briefly is the story of Operation 'Freshman', an ill-fated gliderborne attempt to destroy the Vemork plant, which was launched on 17th November 1942 from an airfield in Scotland.

The town of Rjukan and the village of Vemork stand on opposite sides of an inland fjord formed by a deep mountain valley. The Gau'sta overlooking Vemork towers up to 1,883 metres and on both sides of the valley the steep slopes below 1,000 metres are covered in trees. The Vemork plant was built 300 metres up the side of the mountain and was only reached after a steep, difficult climb. When it was decided to mount the operation with gliders a suitable LZ was chosen a night's march from the target and one of the RAF 'Eureka' signals devices was planted in the area by agents. The soldiers who volunteered for the raid were airborne engineers from the 9th Field Company and the 261st Field Park Company. Two separate parties commanded by Lieutenants A. C. Allen and D. A. Methuen were carried in two Horsa gliders, one piloted by Staff Sergeant M. F. Strathdee and Sergeant P. Doig and the other by Pilot Officer Davis and Sergeant Pilot Fraser, both of the Royal Australian Air Force. The tug aircraft provided were Halifax bombers under the command of Group Captain T. B. Cooper of No 38 Wing.

The full details of the Vemork Raid will never be known. Both Halifax-Horsa combinations took off from their departure airfield late on the 17th on a north-easterly course across the North Sea to Norway. The approach to Rjukan, which lies 120 miles inland from Stavanger and eighty-two miles due west of Oslo, would have taken the aircraft over what even in daylight would be considered difficult map-reading terrain. The meteorological report was excellent but after crossing the Norwegian coast on correct bearings the aircraft flew into a blizzard.

In one of the Halifax tugs the 'Rebecca' radio unit failed to make contact with the 'Eureka' ground beacon and the pilot realising that he had insufficient petrol to prolong the search for the LZ turned for home. At this point the tow rope snapped and the glider crash-landed in thick snow on a mountain-side killing three of the troops on impact. The pilot of the Halifax cleared the mountain top but collided head-on with the next range and all crew members were killed. The survivors of the glider party were quickly rounded up by German troops and executed by a firing squad within a few hours. The second Halifax located the right area but the inter-communication link would not work and the glider cast off prematurely diving blindly through dense cloud into high ground. The tug crew could do nothing to help and so returned safely to base. Of the seventeen men on board the second glider, eight were killed on landing, four were injured and five climbed out of the wreckage unhurt. The injured men were conveyed to Stavanger hospital where they were administered poison by German doctors. The fit men were put in a nearby prison and two months later shot by the Gestapo.

The North African Campaign

Within three days of the Allied invasion of French North Africa (Operation 'Torch') on 8th November 1942, General Eisenhower's task force had gained Morocco and most of Algeria and were driving eastwards as planned to the Tunisian frontier. Although an American airborne attempt on the first day to capture two French airfields – La Senìa and Tafaroui – near Oran had failed, the initial Anglo-American seaborne landings at Safi, Casablanca, Port Lyautey, Oran and Algiers had been completely successful. In spite of the threat now posed by the Germans to the Vichy-controlled zone of Metropolitan France, Admiral Darlan had little option on the third day but to formally surrender the French garrison in Algeria to General Mark Clark. By then Lieutenant-General Anderson's British First Army supported by all available US units on the eastern sector of the landings had overrun airfields in Eastern Algeria on which air support could be centred for the drives to Bizerta and Tunis. The Axis High Command on 9th November sent heavy reinforcements by air and sea to Tunisia, which by the end of November numbered 15,000 men (two-thirds of them air-landed) supported by tanks, artillery and an ever increasing air force. Allied and Axis forces first clashed in strength on 16th November at Beja eighty miles west of Tunis.

After taking off from Cornwall on 9th November, Lieutenant-Colonel Geoffrey Pine-Coffin's 3rd Parachute Battalion flew via Gibraltar to Maison Blanche, an airfield twelve miles from Algiers. The airborne contingent consisted of two companies, plus the Mortar Platoon, HQ Company and a field ambulance. The remainder of Brigadier Flavell's 1st Parachute Brigade – the 1st, 2nd and balance of the 3rd Battalions – which had left England on 1st November, arrived by sea in Algiers eleven days later; and after surviving a heavy bombing raid on their transport ships lying at berth in the harbour, the troops marched out of Algiers in column to a village called St Charles. Pine-Coffin was informed at Gibraltar on the 10th that his battalion after air-landing at Maison Blanche must prepare immediately for parachute operations. One Dakota crashed into the sea *en route* from Gibraltar but all the occupants were rescued by a passing American ship. On the morning of the 11th and only a few hours after their arrival at Maison Blanche, twenty-nine Dakotas bearing 360 parachutists were ready to take off again.

Anderson informed Pine-Coffin later that day that the battalion was to seize Bone airfield along the coast on the Algerian side of the frontier with Tunisia. Speed was of the essence as a *Fallschirmjäger* battalion stationed in Tunis was thought to have the same objective in mind; but as the American Dakota pilots had not dropped parachute troops before, it was decided to forgo the idea of a night operation and delay the fly-in until the dawn of the following day. At 08.30 hours on the 12th after an eventful

flight along the coast when one of their number went down into the sea the Dakotas were over the target area. The drop was accurate but the unaccustomed atmospheric conditions played havoc with parachute performance and twelve men were seriously injured on landing. One man was killed after a parachute failure and three died in the wreckage of the Dakota at sea.

The enemy was nowhere in sight but while the parachutists were taking up defensive positions the DZ was invaded by a horde of friendly but inquisitive Arabs. Confusion reigned and the Arabs could not be prevented from pinching battalion property; the silk parachutes being especially prized amongst the bountiful gifts from heaven. A few hours later the airfield was dive-bombed by Stukas but the position was relieved by No. 6 Commando landing from the sea and the runway was cleared for the arrival of a squadron of Spitfires. Unknown to the British parachute battalion the *Fallschirmjäger* approaching the airfield in Junkers aircraft actually observed the drop but turned away and flew back to Tunis.

Allied strategy in French North Africa was based on the capture of the ports of Bizerta and Tunis and an early link-up in Eastern Tunisia with Montgomery's Eighth Army advancing in November from El Alamein towards Benghazi in Libya. The contours of the Tell region of Northern Tunisia decline gradually in height from the Atlas mountains to the narrow seaboard between Tabarka and Bizerta. The lines of advance into Northern Tunisia lay along two principal routes. The northern coastal road running through hilly country in the area of the Jebel Aboid to Tamera and Bizerta and the southern road from Souk Ahras that passes through Beja to Tunis. The road junction town of Beja in the centre effectively commanded the

Destination Souk el Arba. Men of Hill's 3rd Parachute Battalion wait expectantly for the order to 'prepare for action'. Note the knee pads which were often worn in the North African and Middle Eastern theatres.

approach to both Bizerta and Tunis. Inland from the coastal strip the hills are rocky and barren but the valleys and plains are fertile; and between December and March the rains are liable to turn the ploughed earth into a sea of brown mud. On 15th November the First Army was heading for Beja.

After capturing Bone airfield the 3rd Battalion rejoined 1st Parachute Brigade now on stand-by at Maison Blanche. When the First Army attacked on the 15th, the 1st Battalion (Hill) was ordered to drop on the Souk el Arba plain and capture the road junction at Beja and the airfield, and to persuade the French garrison to join up with the Allies. At the same time American paratroopers were to drop on airfields nearer at hand at Tebessa and Youks les Bains. The Americans jumped as planned but when the 1st Battalion arrived over Beja on the 15th the town was obscured by cloud and the drop was cancelled. The battalion took off again from Maison Blanche on the 16th with orders to be less cautious in their tactical approach but the weather was good and James Hill flying in the leading Dakota took a good look at the terrain before putting his men down near the village of Souk el Arba. The drop was unopposed but as at Bone aroused great interest in the Arab population: the parachutists were greeted also by French native troops; and the RAMC element set up a medical station in a small French hospital to treat injuries. Hill borrowed a fleet of old buses and the battalion moved off in comfort spending the night in a bivouac outside Beja.

Hill resolved on the following day to 'show the flag' to the French garrison by parading in the town and the local commander duly impressed by the display of apparent strength agreed to cooperate with the British Army. The 1st Battalion immediately dug in around the town and one company was in part detached to test the French reaction further north in the village

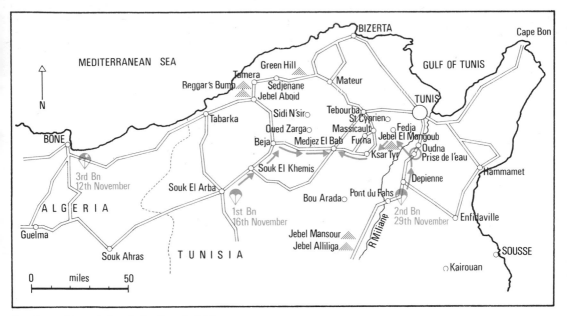

1st Parachute Brigade in North Africa.

of Sidi N'Sir. After meeting with a friendly reception from Senegalese troops in the village, Cleasby-Thompson's 'R' Company engaging in guerrilla tactics destroyed an enemy column on the road to Mateur. Hill moved the 1st Battalion up to Sidi N'Sir and joined by the black Senegalese warriors on the night of 23rd–24th November led a moonlight assault on an Italian tank laager at Gué hill. The attack was preceded by a mortar bombardment but the explosives intended for the tanks accidentally exploded killing twenty-seven sappers. Finding no tanks at the foot of the hill 'R' and 'S' Companies supported by the French colonials charged to the top to find a mixed force of German and Italian machine-gunners. Those defenders who stayed to fight and did not surrender were killed with the bayonet. When the CO reached the hill top he found only three tanks and they were dug-in as gun positions; he obtained the surrender of the crews by tapping on the gun turrets with a stick, and then fell hit in the chest by automatic fire. His life was saved by an airborne surgeon operating at the hospital at Beja.

On 25th November General Eisenhower moved his HQ to Algiers; and on the 28th an Anglo-US force reached Djedeida only twelve miles from Tunis. This was the climax of the advance for now heavy rains set in turning the Allied airstrips into quagmires and grounding the aircraft. Supply routes became impassable and only the barest necessities reached the forward areas. In a last desperate attempt to win the race for Tunisia before the wet season developed, 2nd Parachute Battalion was alerted to jump near Depienne airfield, south of Tunis. John Frost, whose exploits at Bruneval had won him the Military Cross, now commanded the battalion. The operational plan was coordinated with 6th Armoured Division's proposed thrust for Tunis; the immediate airborne objectives being to destroy enemy aircraft on the ground and to capture the airfield.

The CO received his orders on the 28th and the following evening the 2nd Battalion jumped from Dakotas on to a ploughed field near Pont du Fahs some twelve miles from the target. After marching through the night Frost discovered that Depienne airfield was abandoned and so he decided to push on to Oudna airfield on the outskirts of Tunis. No enemy planes were to be seen there either and the battalion after clashing with German patrols withdrew to a small watering place called Prise de l'eau. The British troops were assured by the French civilians and the Arabs that the Axis troops were falling back on Tunis. This information was unfortunately not true. German troops after attacking at Djedeida were even then driving the Allies back to Medjez el Bab. On 1st December Eisenhower halted his forces along the eastern edge of the mountains from Medjez el Bab in the north through Ousseltia and Faid to Gafsa in the south. 2nd Parachute Battalion was stranded fifty miles behind the lines!

The signal informing Frost of the postponement of the Allied advance was received at dawn on the 1st and his predicament was emphasised when a German column was seen approaching from Oudna. An attempted ambush was partially successful but the parachute troops got the worst of their encounter with a second column. An NCO captured by the Germans was sent to the CO pointing out that the British troops were surrounded. The battalion commander at once ordered a fighting withdrawal. Leaving a small party to protect the wounded from hostile Arabs, the battalion began its retreat. In the afternoon 'B' and 'C' Companies with 'A' Company in reserve stopped to form defensive positions based on two small hills. German infantry dismounting from lorries put in a series of determined attacks supported by tanks and covered by heavy machine-gun, mortar and artillery fire. The outcome of the enemy onslaught that continued until evening was devastating; 'C' Company was virtually eliminated, and when the retreat was resumed the medical officer remained behind to look after a large party of wounded.

Moving slowly over hill paths and across ploughed land, streams and ditches the survivors of the battalion were pursued all the way to the safety of the Allied outposts. As the men were now completely exhausted the CO ordered evasive tactics to conserve the rapidly diminishing supply of ammunition. The French farmers were friendly and gave the small groups of parachutists food but warned them that the Arabs in the area were treacherous. Late on 3rd December the troops dispirited by the growing number of casualties sustained in tough encounters with the enemy were overjoyed to meet an American scout car. That evening, 180 men, less than twenty-five per cent. of the full battalion strength, marched through the lines to Medjez el Bab.

There were no more airborne operations in North Africa, partly because of the weather but more so because the three parachute battalions were wanted in the line. The 3rd Battalion entrained from Maison Blanche for Beja and was quickly despatched to participate in the sixteen-day struggle to hold Hunt's Gap; later the same troops were sent to the northern coastal road to take part in the attack on Green Hill. Advocates of the airborne method argued that had the Parachute Regiment been allowed to deploy as a brigade at the beginning of the campaign, they

might well have spearheaded the First Army's arrival in Tunis by the end of November.

A Vickers machine-gunner in action in North Africa.

Throughout February 1st Parachute Brigade held the Bou Arada sector on the right of the line. On the night of 2nd–3rd February Pearson's 1st Battalion was instructed to capture the rugged heights of the Jebel Mansour. The assault was led by 'R' and 'T' Companies protected on the left flank by a company of the French Foreign Legion; 'S' Company was to consolidate the gain at the hill top. The hill was quickly captured and so was the Jebel Alliliga the same night. But shells and mortar bombs rained down upon the parachute troops and legionnaires for three days, and the enemy counter-attacked in strength on the 5th preceded by Stuka dive-bombers. The well-constructed defensive positions were clearly untenable; relief by the Guards Brigade had not materialised, and ammunition supplies were practically exhausted. When Alastair Pearson was reluctantly given permission to withdraw, casualties numbered about 200 killed and wounded.

Elsewhere on the Bou Arada sector the 2nd and 3rd Battalions were engaged in containing attacks and probes by German, Austrian and

1st Parachute
Brigade in North
Africa. The advance
to Bizerta.

Italian troops. At the beginning of March the Allies regained the offensive but the Axis forces still held the initiative on the coastal strip. 1st Parachute Brigade on 5th March moved north to help defend the Tamera Valley. The enemy for the most part occupied the hills and directed intensive and prolonged artillery fire on the ground below. The thick woods assisted infiltration by both sides and ground was lost and won after savage infantry duels.

On the northern flank the British 5th Corps offensive on 17th March recaptured Sedjenane, removing the threat to Medjez el Bab. Leading the advance with the 139th Infantry Brigade, 1st Parachute Brigade on the left went forward to clear the road to Bizerta. The 1st and 2nd Battalions with Goum irregulars under command crossed their start-line in the vicinity of the Jebel Aboid. Replacements for casualties were supplied by the 3rd Battalion from the rear area. The parachute troops had progressed beyond Sedjenane to within twenty miles of Bizerta when on 14th April an American division passed through 1st Parachute Brigade in the line of advance. The brigade had at last been relieved and moved back to Tabarka to rest. The US 2nd Corps had met Montgomery's Eighth Army on the 7th at Gafsa whereupon the Allies closed in on Tunis. On 13th May organised Axis resistance in North Africa ceased.

In June, 1st Parachute Brigade now commanded by Brigadier G. W.

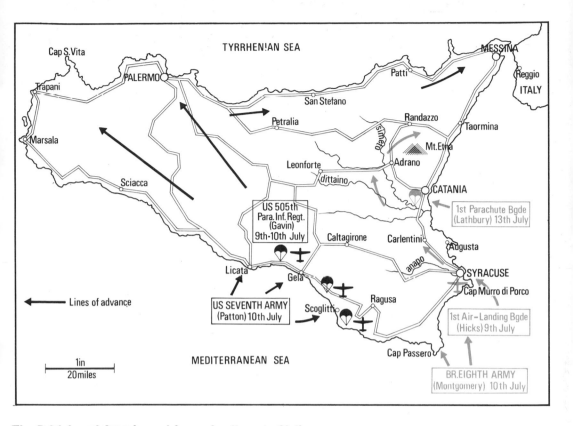

Map labels:

TYRRHENIAN SEA

Cap S.Vita
PALERMO
Trapani
Marsala
Sciacca
San Stefano
Petralia
Patti
MESSINA
Reggio
ITALY
Randazzo
Taormina
Mt.Etna
Leonforte
Adrano
CATANIA
dittaino
Simeto
1st Parachute Bgde
(Lathbury) 13th July
US 505th
Para.Inf.Regt.
(Gavin)
9th-10th July
Caltagirone
Carlentini
Augusta
Licata
Gela
SYRACUSE
Cap Murro di Porco
Lines of advance
Ragusa
anapo
US SEVENTH ARMY
(Patton) 10th July
Scoglitti
1st Air–Landing Bgde
(Hicks) 9th July
1 in
20 miles
MEDITERRANEAN SEA
Cap Passero
BR.EIGHTH ARMY
(Montgomery) 10th July

The British and American airborne landings in Sicily.

Lathbury assembled near Mascara south of Oran. The '*roten Teufeln*' or 'red devils' as the Germans had called them had forged an awesome reputation in battle. The Parachute Regiment accepted their new name as a compliment coming as it did from such a tough adversary. The price paid by the Parachute Regiment for its North African battle honours amounted to 1,700 men killed, wounded and missing.

The Invasion of Sicily

General Lathbury's battle-tested brigade was in April joined from England at Mascara by the 2nd Parachute Brigade (Down) and the 1st (Air-Landing) Brigade (Hicks). The operational strength of Hopkinson's 1st Airborne Division was later supplemented by 'Shan' Hackett's 4th Parachute Brigade arriving by sea from Libya. Major-General Matthew B. Ridgway's US 82nd Division was already busily training in North Africa for airborne operations in Sicily. The 82nd Division consisted of Colonel Reuben Tucker's 504th and Colonel Jim Gavin's 505th Parachute Infantry Regiments and the 325th Glider Infantry Regiment. 'Hoppy' Hopkinson persuaded General Montgomery that 1st Airborne Division was also needed in Sicily and that gliderborne and not parachute troops should lead the assault.

The Allied forces in the Mediterranean were ready for the invasion of Sicily by early July. Under the supreme command of General Eisenhower, the land forces consisted of the Fifteenth Army Group under the direction of General Alexander comprising the United States Seventh Army, commanded by Lieutenant-General George S. Patton, Jr, and the British Eighth Army under General Montgomery. The Allied troops taking part in the seaborne landings included three American and three British divisions plus one Canadian division and an independent British brigade. Powerful naval and air forces were allotted to cover 3,000 invasion ships and craft. The assault from the sea was to be preceded by American parachute landings near Gela and by British glider landings near Syracuse.

The capture of Sicily was planned as a pincer movement with the Seventh Army disembarking on the west coast between Licata and Scoglitti and the Eighth Army on the east coast south of Syracuse. Jim Gavin's reinforced 505th Regiment was to seize the high ground (Piano Lupo) in the Gela area to prevent the enemy from reaching the American bridgehead; and 'Pip' Hicks 1st (Air-Landing) Brigade was to capture the Ponte Grande canal bridge commanding the approach to the city of Syracuse. A further attack on the harbour itself was intended as a diversion. The task of seizing the bridge by *coup de main* was allocated to Major Ballinger's 'C' Company, 2nd South Staffords, landing on two LZs near the canal. The main body of the battalion commanded by Lieutenant-Colonel McCardie was to land on a third LZ south of the canal and move north to consolidate in the area of the bridge. Lieutenant-Colonel Britten's 1st Bn the Border Regiment was to touch down with the South Staffords; assist if necessary in holding the bridge and move on to the harbour.

The worst problem facing the airborne planners was that of the allocation of the Dakotas belonging to XII Troop Carrier Command. But differences of opinion between Ridgway and Browning seem to have been solved as on D-1 (9th July) the Air-Landing Brigade took off in the evening from Tunisian airfields to launch Operation 'Husky', the Allied invasion of Sicily. The 2,000 British troops of the glider battalions were followed into the air shortly afterwards by Gavin's 4,400 American paratroopers. The glider force numbered 137 of the American Wacos and eight Horsas to carry stores and 2-pounders, machine-guns and mortars. Clouds of dust arose as the tow ropes took the strain when their tugs taxied over the airstrips. The British pilots, who had hastily converted on to the Wacos, looked back at their passengers, waved confidently and gave the thumbs up signal.

The success of the glider operation (code-named 'Ladbroke') depended on surprise, and to avoid being picked up by enemy radar, a devious route was followed; the tugs making for Delimara point on the south-east coast of Malta, then turning north-east towards Sicily, passing Cap Passero and from there on to the neighbourhood of Cap Murro di Porco. Two and a half miles short of this promontory the gliders were to be released. Seven of the gliders did not even make it over the North African coastline but about ninety per cent. of the tugs entered the second leg of the journey from Malta with their charges unscathed.

The wind had begun to rise from the south-east before the airborne formation passed Malta but soon it increased to gale proportions. Flying conditions were made worse by the necessity to fly low to escape radar detection. Wind speeds reached forty-five mph but moderated to around thirty mph when the tugs approached Cap Passero. Several adverse factors led to about sixty per cent. of the gliders being prematurely parted from the tugs. The sparse light of the quarter-moon was of little help to the tug navigators but as the tug-glider combinations flew along the coast a wall of dust raised by the off-shore wind blotted out the landmarks completely. Many of the tugs turned away too soon, the glider pilots blindly slipping their tow ropes before crash-landing in the sea. The more fortunate of the troops clinging to the floating wooden wreckages were picked up by the passing assault craft; others including the brigade commander swam for the shore. Altogether 252 men were drowned. Only fifty-two of the gliders made landfall, and only twelve of them landed anywhere near the target.

The troops who came successfully to ground were widely scattered on the southern reaches of Syracuse. Major Ballinger, who was to lead the Ponte Grande assault, was killed immediately after stepping out of his glider but Lieutenant Withers and the fourteen men of the South Staffords who landed nearest the bridge took the objective before midnight. German demolition charges were removed from the bridge. The garrison was increased by small parties during the night and at first light on the 10th the mixed force of South Staffords and Borders amounted to seven officers and eighty other ranks; in addition to their small arms, they had one 3-in mortar, one 2-in mortar and four Bren guns. The bridge was shelled throughout the morning and casualties steadily mounted. At 15.00 hours only fifteen men remained unwounded; and then, their ammunition spent, the position was overrun by the enemy. Half an hour later a Border officer having eluded the attackers met patrols of the 17th Infantry Brigade coming up the road from the beaches; an attack was at once launched and the bridge re-taken before it could be destroyed.

In Tunisia 1st and 2nd Parachute Brigades were awaiting their orders to jump in Sicily. When news of the costly success at the Ponte Grande bridge and the fall of Syracuse was received, contingency plans for the employment of 2nd Parachute Brigade near Augusta were cancelled. On 13th July 1st Parachute Brigade received the order confirming that their attack on the Primosole bridge to secure the line of advance to Catania was to take place that night.

The 1st, 2nd and 3rd Battalions emplaned on the evening of 13th July in 105 Dakota and eleven Albemarle aircraft. In addition, Halifaxes and Stirlings towed eight Waco and eleven Horsa gliders carrying gunners, anti-tank guns, sappers and field ambulancemen. Gerald Lathbury's plan (code-named 'Fustian') was to land on four DZs and two LZs all west of the main road from Syracuse to Catania. The Primosole bridge spanning the River Simeto is located a few miles south of Catania. The 1st Battalion was to approach the bridge from both sides and the 3rd (now Yeldham) and the 2nd were to secure the high ground north of the Simeto River and south of the Gornalunga Canal. Flying in V-formation the aircraft followed the route taken via Malta by the glider brigade. Anti-aircraft gunners on board the invasion ships opened fire mistaking the Dakotas for torpedo-carrying aircraft. Two were shot down and nine – after sustaining heavy damage – were forced to turn back.

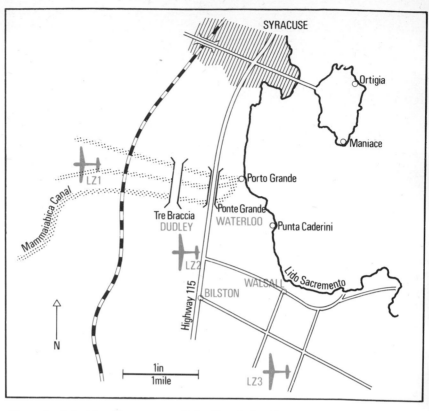

The scheduled landing zones of the South Staffords near the Ponte Grande bridge.

The close formations were broken up and it was now the German and Italian anti-aircraft gunners who brought fire to bear on the low-flying aircraft. Ten more turned back and thirty-seven crashed into the sea and on to the beaches. The pilots of the surviving planes dropped their paratroopers or advised their glider colleagues to cast-off whenever and wherever they could. Of the 1,900 men of 1st Parachute Brigade that had taken off from North Africa, only about 250 men from the 1st and 3rd Battalions reached the Primosole bridge.

Brigadier Lathbury assigned the command of the bridge defensive positions to Lieutenant-Colonel Pearson, who ordered the majority of his troops to dig in on the north side of the river. Three anti-tank guns, two 3-in mortars, light machine-guns and a Vickers machine-gun were sited and the road mined. Earlier in the day units of Heidrich's 1st Parachute Division had flown from Rome and parachuted into the same area. A group of *Fallschirmjäger* were rallied during the night to evict the red devils from the Primosole bridge. Pearson's force strongly resisted but when tanks, infantry and a self-propelled gun were brought up from Catania to reinforce the German paratroopers the British troops were obliged to retire. No word had been received by Lathbury at this stage from John Frost's 2nd Battalion operating in the hills south of the river. Frost had made contact, however, with the 4th Armoured Brigade and the

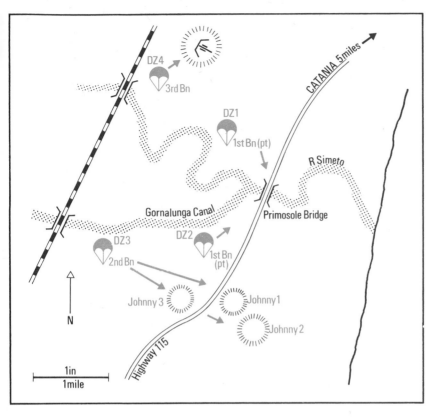

4th Parachute
Battalion in Italy.
The location is
Venafro on the
Cassino sector.

**The dispositions of 1st Parachute Brigade in the area of the
Primosole bridge.**

battalion was moving up the road with the tanks to the bridge.

Several forceful attacks by the British armour, the paratroopers and other infantry units were held by the Axis troops. Finally after a two-day battle their resistance was broken and at dawn on the 16th men of the Durham Light Infantry probing forward found that the defenders had gone. At the time of the Primosole action Montgomery was already shifting the main weight of his attack westwards along the Simeto River to Adrano. In so doing the Eighth Army swung to the left around Mount Etna meeting the Americans completing the pincer from the west at Randazzo. Messina fell on 17th August and the Sicilian campaign fought against two German and eleven Italian divisions was over. By this time 1st Parachute Brigade had embarked at Syracuse for its base in North Africa. Casualties suffered by 1st Airborne Division in Sicily numbered 454 dead (including fifty-seven glider pilots), 240 wounded and 102 missing.

1st Airborne in Italy

In late August 1943 the whole of the 1st Airborne Division was concentrated in Tunisia at Sousse and in its neighbourhood. On 19th August Marshal Badoglio established contact with General Eisenhower to negotiate an Italian surrender without the knowledge of the Germans. The Italian unconditional surrender was signed at Cassibile in Sicily on 3rd September and announced five days later. The fall of Mussolini had opened new prospects for the impending Allied invasion of the Italian mainland. On 3rd September the Canadian 1st and British 5th Divisions landed in the 'toe' of Italy around Reggio; on the 9th, Mark Clark's Fifth Army comprising the US 6th Corps and the British 10th Corps went ashore at two points in the Gulf of Salerno; on the same day Hopkinson's 1st Airborne Division sailing from Bizerta arrived in Taranto harbour.

The vanguard of the landing at Taranto was provided by 2nd and 4th Parachute Brigades with 1st Parachute Brigade following on behind. The disembarkation of the division would have been uneventful but for the disaster that befell the 6th (Royal Welch) Battalion. HMS *Abdiel* bearing 400 men of the battalion and some support troops hit a mine in the harbour and sank within two minutes. Fifty-eight men were killed and 154 injured. Hackett's 4th Brigade led the advance from Taranto to capture Moltala. It was when the 10th Battalion was in action against the German defences at Castellaneta that the Divisional Commander, Major-General Hopkinson, fell mortally wounded. The command of the division until his transfer to India was held by Major-General Eric·Down.

Although the Allies made good progress in both west and east the fall of Rome was far from imminent. On the east coast on the airborne sector Down was determined to keep the initiative; the 10th and 156th Battalions were constantly sending out patrols and on 16th September the 10th Battalion took Gioia airfield. In the nine days that had elapsed since coming ashore at Taranto 4th Parachute Brigade had seen some sharp fighting but casualties had been slight. The Air-Landing Brigade relieved the 4th Brigade and entered Foggia. 1st Parachute Brigade in the line at Altamura in October mounted a minor parachute drop involving one officer and seven other ranks on the east coast north of Pescara with the object of guiding escaped Allied prisoners through the lines. By November 1943 1st Airborne Division was withdrawn from the Italian theatre and returned to England to prepare for the invasion of North West Europe.

2nd Independent Parachute Brigade

Brigadier C. H. V. Pritchard's 2nd Parachute Brigade remaining in Italy was declared 'independent' and in theory placed on stand-by to launch airborne operations in support of the Eighth Army. In practice the brigade composed of the 4th, 5th and 6th Battalions plus support units fought on as infantry of the line under General Freyberg's 2nd New Zealand Division. In October the Fifth Army crossed the Volturno river and the German Army pulled back to its defensive strongholds in the Abruzzese mountains. The 'winter line', known also as the Gustave line, ran athwart the peninsula following generally the courses of the Sangro, Liri and Garigliano rivers. At the end of November the Eighth Army was placed along the Sangro river and the Fifth Army was lodged at the entrance of the Liri Valley. Overlooking the Liri from the east and crowned by a village and monastery rose the towering heights of Monte Cassino. After advancing across the Sangro on the left flank of the Eighth Army to Orsogna, 2nd Parachute Brigade was in action for four months on the coastal sector. After a rest period in Naples the brigade was sent in March 1944 with the New Zealanders to the Cassino area and was engaged in patrol work along the Rapido river.

In June, 2nd Independent Parachute Brigade was alerted at a rest camp at Salerno to take part in Operation 'Anvil', the invasion of the South of France. At last the brigade was to take part in a major airborne operation. The 'red berets' were to form part of the Allied airborne force, which was to drop inland from the coast with the object of advancing up the Rhône valley to meet the Allied armies spreading out from Normandy. Operation 'Anvil' did not take place until August but the 2nd Brigade remained on stand-by in Italy from June onwards. The brigade actually launched a small parachute raid from Salerno on 1st June. Three officers and fifty-seven men were dropped from three Dakotas near Torricella in the rear of the Germans then withdrawing from Rome towards the Pisa-Rimini (Gothic) line. The parachutists acting in three guerrilla groups successfully blocked a supply road for over a week.

6th Airborne in Normandy

On 24th February 1944 6th Airborne Division was placed under the command of I Corps for Operation 'Overlord', the Allied invasion of North-West Europe. The British assault from the sea was to be on a two corps front, the right being XXX Corps and the left I Corps. The attack was to be led by the 50th Division landing on 'Gold' beach at Asnelles; the (Canadian) 3rd Division followed by the 51st Division on 'Juno' beach north of Caen; and the 3rd Division on 'Sword' beach west of Ouistreham. 6th Airborne Division was to come in first landing east of the Orne river. Summarily, General Gale was to form a lodgement on twenty-four square miles of French soil between the Orne and Dives rivers and defend the left flank of the invasion forces.

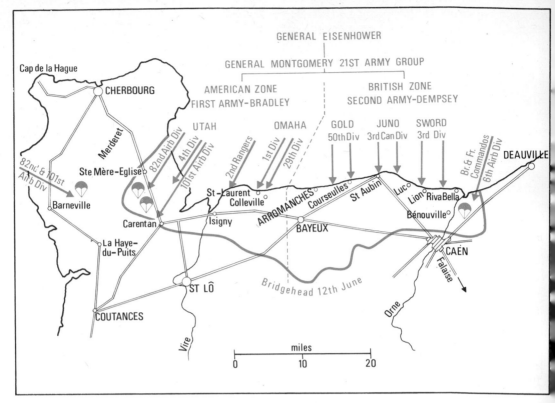

Operation 'Neptune', 6th June 1944. The Allied airborne landings and the assault beaches.

The divisional commander allocated his tasks as follows:

5th Parachute Brigade (Poett): the capture of the bridges over the Canal de Caen and the River Orne at Bénouville and Ranville.

The two bridges stand less than a mile apart on the parallel courses of the canal and river that meet the coast east of Ouistreham. The Bénouville bridge lay three miles inland from 'Sword' beach; unless the two crossings were taken intact the canal and river presented double obstacles to the 3rd Division moving up from the beachhead. The job of seizing the bridges was allotted to a *coup de main* party landing in gliders five hours before the dawn (P-5 hours). Shortly after the glider landings the parachute troops were to drop in brigade strength to take over the bridges and establish defensive positions in the surrounding area of villages, orchards and farm land.

The importance of the canal and river crossings was further emphasised by the plan to bring in the bulk of Brigadier the Hon. Hugh Kindersley's *6th (Air-Landing) Brigade* near Ranville on the afternoon of D-Day.

3rd Parachute Brigade (Hill): the destruction of the coastal battery at Merville and the bridges at Varaville, Robehomme, Bures and Troarn.

The brigade was to land simultaneously with the 5th Brigade.

The Merville battery faced north-west from high ground overlooking the

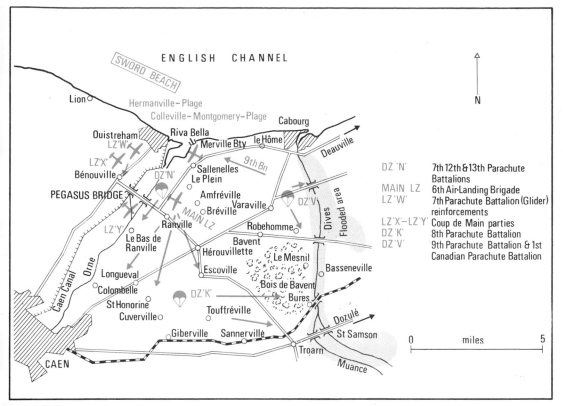

6th Airborne Division's assault on D-Day. The positions between the Caen canal and the Dives river.

mouth of the Orne. The battery's heavy-calibre guns housed in reinforced concrete emplacements were capable of inflicting havoc on the invasion craft; the guns must be silenced at P-30 minutes before the daylight exposed the invasion fleet off 'Sword' beach.

The purpose of destroying the bridges was to seal off the exposed left flank and moreover to prevent enemy reinforcements from passing south of the Bénouville-Ranville-Le Bas de Ranville positions and reaching the town of Caen. (Three roads and one railway line passed through this area.) James Hill, who had by far the largest share of the terrain, was also to seize the ridge Le Plein-Le Mesnil-Troarn. This ridge ran diagonally across the divisional zone from north to east and dominated the Dives river line and the east-west lines of communication. Hill was later to concentrate his brigade south of Le Mesnil and Robehomme in the woods and orchards of the Bois de Bavent.

The disposition and strength of the enemy forces along the French coast was known to the Allied Supreme Command. Field-Marshal Erwin Rommel's Army Group B – the Seventh and Fifteenth Armies – defended Brittany, Normandy and the Pas de Calais. Hausser's Seventh Army faced the invasion beaches; the boundary line between the two armies actually running through General Gale's zone of operations. Rommel had directed most of his efforts to building coast defences. Behind the beaches and cliff

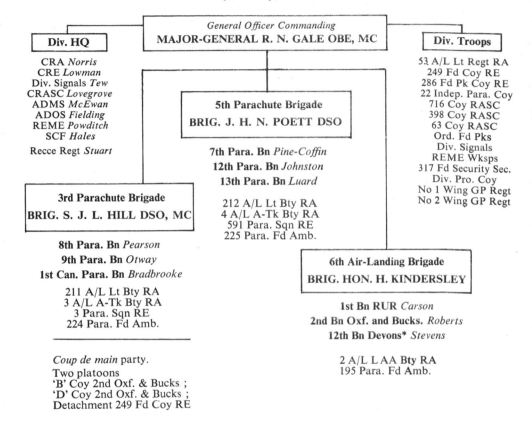

Order of Battle
6th Airborne Division: Operation 'Neptune'
Normandy, D-Day, 6th June 1944

General Officer Commanding
MAJOR-GENERAL R. N. GALE OBE, MC

Div. HQ

CRA *Norris*
CRE *Lowman*
Div. Signals *Tew*
CRASC *Lovegrove*
ADMS *McEwan*
ADOS *Fielding*
REME *Powditch*
SCF *Hales*

Recce Regt *Stuart*

Div. Troops

53 A/L Lt Regt RA
249 Fd Coy RE
286 Fd Pk Coy RE
22 Indep. Para. Coy
716 Coy RASC
398 Coy RASC
63 Coy RASC
Ord. Fd Pks
Div. Signals
REME Wksps
317 Fd Security Sec.
Div. Pro. Coy
No 1 Wing GP Regt
No 2 Wing GP Regt

5th Parachute Brigade
BRIG. J. H. N. POETT DSO

7th Para. Bn *Pine-Coffin*
12th Para. Bn *Johnston*
13th Para. Bn *Luard*

212 A/L Lt Bty RA
4 A/L A-Tk Bty RA
591 Para. Sqn RE
225 Para. Fd Amb.

3rd Parachute Brigade
BRIG. S. J. L. HILL DSO, MC

8th Para. Bn *Pearson*
9th Para. Bn *Otway*
1st Can. Para. Bn *Bradbrooke*

211 A/L Lt Bty RA
3 A/L A-Tk Bty RA
3 Para. Sqn RE
224 Para. Fd Amb.

6th Air-Landing Brigade
BRIG. HON. H. KINDERSLEY

1st Bn RUR *Carson*
2nd Bn Oxf. and Bucks. *Roberts*
12th Bn Devons* *Stevens*

2 A/L L AA Bty RA
195 Para. Fd Amb.

Coup de main party.
Two platoons
'B' Coy 2nd Oxf. & Bucks ;
'D' Coy 2nd Oxf. & Bucks ;
Detachment 249 Fd Coy RE

*'C' Coy only. The remainder of 12th Devons arrived by sea on D-Day + 1.

tops infantry divisions with combat groups held in reserve for counter-attacks were allocated to contiguous sectors of the coastline. In the rear of these first-line defences strong, mobile Panzer and SS divisions were ready to deploy at short notice anywhere to contain a break-through. 6th Airborne Division's immediate concern east of the Orne was the 711th Infantry Division.

Nos 38 and 46 Groups possessed 450 Albemarles, Stirlings, Halifaxes and Dakotas for the British airborne operation. 6,000 parachute and glider assault troops were to be landed between midnight and the dawn of D-Day; the aircraft returning to their airfields in southern England to lift 3,000 men of the main glider force later the same day. Air Chief Marshal Sir Trafford Leigh-Mallory, the Allied Air supremo, pessimistically predicted fifty per cent. losses of carrier, tug planes and gliders.

On 5th June the pilots were briefed for Operation 'Neptune', the code-name for the Allied airborne and beachhead operations on the Cherbourg-Caen sector. No 38 Group RAF (Hollinghurst) was based on airfields at Brize Norton, Tarrant Rushton, Fairford, Keevil and Harwell. This group was responsible for lifting 5th Parachute Brigade and towing the majority of the gliders. 3rd Parachute Brigade was assigned to No 46 Group RAF (Darvall) at Down Ampney, Blake Hill Farm and Broadwell.

At 23.03 hours on 5th June six Albemarle aircraft bearing sixty men of the 22nd Independent Parachute Company took off from Harwell to launch the invasion of France.

Almost as soon as the Pathfinders were airborne six gliders bearing a party of Oxf. and Bucks and Royal Engineers set off for the Caen canal and Orne bridges. At three minutes to midnight the two parachute brigades took off in their transport planes and headed for the French coast. Later an assault party from 9th Parachute Battalion took off in three gliders to make a pinpoint crash-landing on the Merville battery. The night sky soon throbbed with the sound of over a thousand aircraft carrying the British 6th and the American 82nd and 101st Airborne Divisions to leap-frog Hitler's Atlantic Wall. The moon was screened for most of the way by grey cloud; light rain smeared the cockpit windows. More gliders carrying equipment followed the mainstream of the division. The take-off of the first lift was finally concluded when shortly after midnight sixty-eight Horsas took to the air with Div HQ, a field ambulance, reinforcement troops of 7th Parachute Battalion and an assortment of divisional equipment. Four Hamilcars also flew with this contingent.

At 00.20 hours the Pathfinders dropped on three separate zones: DZ 'N' north-east of Ranville; DZ 'K' west of Troarn and DZ 'V' between the Merville battery and Varaville. The first airborne officers to land in France on D-Day were Captains Tate and Medwood and Lieutenants Latour and Vischer. Five minutes before the drop the six gliders of the *coup de main* force released their tow ropes 5,000 feet above the mouth of the Orne and divided into two parties aiming for the canal bridge (LZ 'X') and the river bridge (LZ 'Y'). After spotting both targets from 3,000 feet Staff Sergeant J. H. Wallwork, the No 1 pilot of the leading glider, making for the canal turned into his line of approach and descended on half-flap before releasing an arrester-parachute and hitting the ground fifty yards from the bridge. Both Wallwork and Ainsworth, the No 2 pilot, were thrown through the cockpit window on to wire entanglements. When they picked themselves up they observed that the other two gliders had followed them in and landed a few yards away.

As the assault party of the Oxf. and Bucks led by Major R. J. Howard raced for the bridge Schmeissers opened up taking the first British casualties. Unperturbed by the machine-gun fire, one platoon overwhelmed the defenders on the far side of the bridge while the others cleared a pillbox and a network of trenches on the near bank. The only German troops who survived were those who ran off to raise the alarm. During the *mêlée* a runner informed Howard that the Orne bridge had been taken unoppo-

5

6   7

8

1 Richard Gale, raised 1st Parachute Brigade, formed and led 6th Airborne Division in Normandy.

2 The Queen talks to a a Canadian paratrooper. James Hill is on the right of the photograph.

3 The Queen with two glider pilots.

4 Lieutenant-Colonel Bradbrooke, CO Canadian Battalion

5 Monty with 8th Parachute Battalion. Left. Major John Marshall. Right. Lieutenant-Colonel Alastair Pearson.

6 D-Day briefing. 22nd Independent Parachute Company, 6th Airborne Division. This photograph was released on 6th June but the censor's scrawl indicated that the map detail must be obscured before publication.

7 Men of the Parachute Regiment prepare for the night drop on D-Day.

8 Pathfinder officers at Harwell on the night of 5th June 1944, prior to take-off in an Albemarle for Normandy. Left to right. Lieutenants Robert de Latour, Donald Wells, John Vischer and Captain Robert Medwood.

sed. Two of the Horsas had landed on target but the third touched down fifteen miles to the east in the Dives valley. Major Howard now formed linked bridgeheads astride the canal and river.

Meanwhile about 2,000 men of 5th Parachute Brigade were disentangling themselves from their parachutes on DZ 'N' near Ranville. The arrival of the Pathfinders had alerted the German defences and when the brigade dropped in a stiffish wind the sky was filled with anti-aircraft shells and tracer bullets. Lieutenant-Colonel Pine-Coffin, commanding 7th Parachute Battalion, collected the troops who had assembled at his rendezvous and moved off to relieve Howard's force. The division had already been warned about the wooden spikes that had been driven into the fields to obstruct glider landings. The spikes, known as 'Rommel's asparagus', were 20ft long by eighteen inches in diameter and some were wired to mines. The airborne sappers' first job was to clear the Ranville area for the main glider landings later in the day. 12th Parachute Battalion (Johnston) after capturing Le Bas de Ranville took up positions covering the village. The 13th Battalion (Luard) occupied Ranville, which was held under heavy shell and mortar fire.

The plan to knock out the Merville battery had been carefully rehearsed by Lieutenant-Colonel T. B. H. Otway's 9th Parachute Battalion in great secrecy near Newbury. The battalion's four companies were assigned as reconnaissance, breaching, assault and reserve parties. The three gliders carrying sappers, equipment and a covering section were scheduled to descend in the neighbourhood of the battery at 04.20 hours when the breaching company was expected to be in position. Otway's battalion commenced dropping with Bradbrooke's 1st Canadian Parachute Battalion shortly before 01.00 hours on DZ 'V' near Varaville. The country around Varaville is flat and low-lying. The town itself forms the tip of a salient of firm ground jutting into marshes west of the River Dives. 3rd Parachute Brigade intended using the marshes as part of the natural flank barrier, but the area had been flooded by the Germans and many of the parachutists went straight into the water.

The Merville battery was garrisoned by 130 men and was sited in an elaborate defensive system. Terence Otway could only find about twenty-five per cent. of his battalion on the DZ but nonetheless resolved to advance. Prior to the attack Lancasters bombed the battery but succeeded

The Allied airborne invasion of the South of France. Dakotas in flight.

101

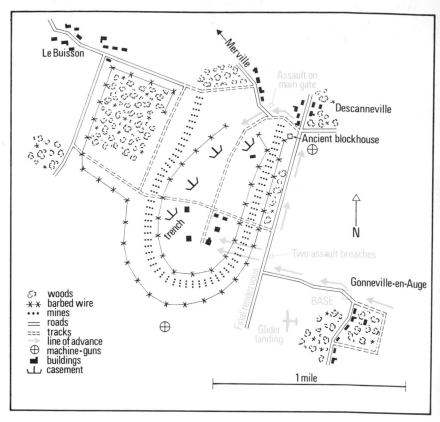

9th Parachute Battalion's attack on the Merville battery.

only in killing most of the recce party and devastating the village of Merville. Of the three gliders that took off from base one broke loose from its tug before crossing the English coast. The other two crossed the Channel at 1,000 feet but the Eureka beacon that should have been planted on the LZ had inadvertently been destroyed and the pilots found the landmarks indistinguishable in the darkness. Staff Sergeant S. G. Bone landed in a field near Merville but did not discover his whereabouts until the following morning. Staff Sergeant D. F. Kerr on the other hand flew low over the target and releasing his arrester-parachute crash-landed in an orchard some 200 yards from the battery site. The glider burst into flames but the occupants escaped only to clash head-on with a German patrol.

These glider troops were instrumental in holding off German reinforcements while Otway's force made the assault. The recce troops had earlier succeeded in cutting a gap through the outer wire and laying tapes. The main party now blew two lanes through the perimeter minefield with Bangalore torpedoes and advanced with sub-machine-guns blazing on the German gunners. Over one hundred of the defenders had fallen before the twenty fit survivors surrendered to the paratroopers. Before daybreak the four heavy guns were spiked as planned with Gammon bombs. As soon as the battery was silenced the captors triumphantly lit yellow 'success' flares and re-assembled to take over some of the high ground at Le Plein before launching an attack on Sallanelles. Otway's battalion had lost seventy men in the attack on the Merville battery.

The dry land west of Varaville consists of orchards and fields divided up by the typical Normandy *bocage*. The Canadian battalion like the 9th had been widely scattered as a general result of the failure of the Eureka beacons. About fifty per cent. of the men arrived at their rendezvous and moved off to capture Varaville and destroy the road bridge. Both objectives were quickly achieved and the road bridge at Robehomme was similarly demolished before the Canadians took up their allotted sector north-west of the Bois de Bavent at Le Mesnil. James Hill and his HQ party having also dropped on DZ 'V' now moved in with the Canadians at Le Mesnil. Hill, who had made a good recovery from his chest wound inflicted in North Africa, was hit again within hours of the drop but continued to direct the brigade operation.

The arrival of 8th Parachute Battalion on DZ 'K' west of the Bures and Troarn bridges had completed the descent of 3rd Parachute Brigade. Alastair Pearson, who had parted from the 1st Battalion after a severe bout of malaria in North Africa, now commanded the Midland battalion. (A Scots farmer and keen TA officer, then aged twenty-nine years, Pearson, an aggressive and skilful battalion commander, was awarded no less than the Military Cross, DSO and three bars during his war-time career.) 8th Parachute Battalion's objectives were two railway bridges over the Dives and an adjacent canal north of Bures and road bridges over the Muance and Dives between Troarn and St Samson. Pearson's battalion strength at the DZ rendezvous was about 180 men. Fortunately a stray RE party replaced the missing sappers but because of the shortage of explosives only two of the bridges were actually destroyed. German troops based on Troarn reacted promptly to the presence of the invaders but were unable to prevent Pearson from forming his lines in the Bois de Bavent.

The gliders that had taken off in the wake of the first lift hit heavy flak from the German coastal defences around Le Havre. Before that time five had perforce landed in England and now three were shot down by the enemy gunners. At approximately 03.00 hours forty-seven Horsas and two Hamilcars appeared over their LZ west of Ranville; fifteen of the original seventy-two gliders being accounted for as missing. The glider pilots after releasing were to land on three strips, which had already been cleared by the sappers of landing spikes and mines and marked by T-shape illuminations. The pilots had no difficulty in spotting the flarepaths; two measuring 1,000 yards by 60 yards and the Hamilcar strip 1,000 yards by 90 yards. Once the gliders were on the ground the most urgent need was for the 7th Battalion reinforcements to join up with Pine-Coffin's hard-pressed advance elements at the Bénouville and Ranville bridges.

Before dawn on 6th June Naval Force 'S', carrying Major-General T. G. Rennie's 3rd Division, and its supporting units, were assembled off the mouth of the Orne. The daylight landing at 07.30 hours was preceded by a devastating two-hour aerial and fleet bombardment concentrated on beaches west of Ouistreham and on heavy coastal batteries to the east. The sound of the guns, which included those of the battleships *Warspite* and *Ramillies*, was sweet music to the airborne troops around Ranville but with the 21st Panzer Division already alerted and closing in, a quick link-up with the seaborne forces was imperative.

The scene at daybreak on the airborne sector presented a bewildering sight to the French civilians. Silken canopies of many colours lay strewn in the fields and draped across the thick hedgerows; parachute harnesses hung limply by their rigging lines from the branches of the apple trees. Empty containers were scattered across the dropping zones and others lay unopened in lanes and ditches. The wide dispersal of the troops on the drop meant that small parties of men were now attempting to locate their battalion areas. The civilians had suffered badly from the bombing at Merville but they were active in giving succour to the wounded and injured parachutists.

'B' Company, 7th Parachute Battalion, at dawn was under heavy attack at the Caen canal bridge. During the day the battalion also occupying Bénouville withstood eight separate counter-attacks and repeated attempts by the enemy to infiltrate its defensive positions. At 10.00 hours a jeep arrived and two officers wearing red berets were seen walking across the bridge; they were General Gale and one of his staff. Three hours later the alert ears of the sentries at the bridge picked up the sound of pipes above the noise of battle. A solitary piper then hove into view followed by Brigadier the Lord Lovat marching at the head of No 1 Commando. The sight of the Commandos in their green berets approaching at the steady pace of a routine route march was a welcome boost to the airborne troops' morale. The arrival of the Commandos – five hours before other seaborne units – was more than a merely satisfying moment for General Gale. The airborne sector had yet to be consolidated but all D-Day objectives had been taken and most importantly a link-up of forces had been achieved.

The main glider landing south-east of Ranville that afternoon involved 250 gliders. These brought in the bulk of Hugh Kindersley's 6th (Air-Landing) Brigade. Flying with this group were the Armoured Reconnaissance Regiment, which was equipped with Tetrarch tanks, Bren carriers and motor bicycles, and the sorely needed guns of the 53rd (Air-Landing) Light Regiment, Royal Artillery. By now the weather had changed for the better and the clouds were high in the sky. Four landing strips had been cleared by the sappers, three for Horsas and one for Hamilcars. The gliders, led by Lieutenant-Colonel Iain Murray, commander No 2 Wing, on the whole made good landings.

General Gale fed the Air-Landing Brigade piecemeal into the battle and the division as a whole was fully deployed by D-Day plus 1. 'A' Company, 12th Bn the Devonshire Regiment ('Parker Force'), which landed with the 7th Parachute Battalion glider contingent, was quickly in action at Hérouvillette. The remainder of the 12th Devons came ashore at Lion-sur-Mer and were led from the beachhead by their CO, Lieutenant-Colonel Stevens, riding a bicycle. The Devons temporarily relieved the Yorkshiremen of 12th Parachute Battalion around Le Bas de Ranville. 1st Bn the Royal Ulster Rifles (Carson) attacked successfully at Longueval but less so at St Honorine. With 2nd Bn the Oxf. and Bucks Light Infantry (Roberts) posted along the narrow ridge from Longueval to Escoville, General Gale was forming a solid block of glider troops to the south of Ranville covering the canal and Orne crossings.

On 7th June units of the 3rd Division took over the Caen canal and

Orne bridges. (The canal crossing was officially renamed 'Pegasus Bridge' and is still known locally by that title to this day.) Although General Gale's life-line from Ouistreham was apparently secure his hold on the Orne-Dives sector was nevertheless precarious. The airborne division effectively held a narrow, 'V'-shaped bridgehead pointing south-eastwards to Troarn with its base on the River Orne at Longueval and Sallanelles. To the north-east of the bridgehead scattered elements of 3rd Parachute Brigade were either holding isolated outposts or trying to locate the brigade positions centred on Le Mesnil. In spite of the destruction of the bridges in the east the German 346th Infantry Division succeeded in crossing the Dives and reaching Bréville. By 10th June three enemy divisions were pressing on the bridgehead: the 711th and 346th on the northern flank and the 21st Panzers with their Panther tanks and '88's' on the southern flank. The most persistent pressure was being exerted along the northern edge of the bridgehead although No 1 Commando (under command of 6th Airborne Division) attacked vigorously on the coast at Franceville Plage.

On the morning of 10th June the Germans put in heavy attacks on Le Plein and on the high ground south of Bréville. The drive from Bréville looked as if it might go straight through the bridgehead from west to east and threaten the flank of the invasion forces. 3rd Parachute Brigade augmented by 5th Bn the Black Watch and backed by 12th Parachute Battalion took the full fury of the onslaught but plugged the gap. A gallant counter-attack by the Black Watch cost the Scots battalion very heavy casualties. On the 12th, the 346th Division tried to break through again and the 3rd Brigade and the Black Watch were again under severe pressure. Some of the 8th Battalion moved up from the Bois de Bavent to fill the depleted Scottish ranks but the break-through was finally prevented when the wounded Brigadier Hill himself went out and personally led a ferocious counter-attack by a company of Canadians.

General Gale knew that his only hope of consolidation east of the Orne lay with blotting out the enemy concentration at Bréville. An attack was to be mounted that night from Amfréville by Johnston's 12th Battalion and Bamfylde's 'D' Company, 12th Devons, supported by the 22nd Independent Parachute Company and covered on both flanks by Sherman tanks of the 13th/18th Hussars. The advance was also to be covered by the guns of the 51st Highland Division. As 'C' Company of the 12th Battalion followed by the Devons formed up on their start-line a deluge of shells from their own covering bombardment fell amongst them causing grievous casualties. Lieutenant-Colonel Johnston and Major Bamfylde were instantly killed and Brigadier the Hon Hugh Kindersley and Lord Lovat, who were there to watch the assault, fell seriously wounded. When the Germans replied to the barrage the whole of Amfréville was set on fire.

As the troops went forward so the Germans dropped curtains of shell and mortar fire across their lines of advance. The two leading companies suffered heavily as did the third ('B' Company). Tanks converged on the village from both sides and 'A' Company after capturing the château moved in to consolidate the gain. The 12th Battalion – at the onset only 300 strong – lost half its numbers in the battle to close the Bréville gap. (When Johnston fell Colonel R. G. Parker, Deputy Commander of the

Air-Landing Brigade, took control and led the battalion into action.) The Battle of Bréville was the turning point in the bitter struggle to secure the Orne bridgehead.

On 14th June the 51st Highland Division took over part of the southern flank of the bridgehead along the ridge from Longueval through St Honorine almost to Escoville. The arrival of the Highlanders did not come a moment too soon for the Ulstermen at St Honorine; the 'Rifles' having been practically surrounded in the village for seven days. The divisional strength since D-Day had been reduced to 6,000 men. Consequently Brigadier Leicester's No 4 Commando was placed under command to fill the empty ranks and partnered No 1 Commando on the northern sector. Hill's 3rd Parachute Brigade was temporarily withdrawn and Poett's 5th Brigade and two of the air-landing battalions were assigned to hold the line in the south. Later after a severe tank battle around Ranville the 49th Division moved in on the left of the 51st Highland Division. General Crerar's 1st Canadian Army on the left of 21st Army Group in mid-July assumed command of British I Corps. General Gale's ranks were further reinforced at that time by the Belgian Brigade (Pirron) and Princess Irene's Royal Netherlands Brigade (de Ruyter Van Stevenick). The airborne division was now getting full gunner support and the Tetrarch tanks of the Recce Regiment were replaced by Cromwells.

A divisional news-sheet entitled *Pegasus Goes to it* (ed Captain Charles Strafford) was first issued to the airborne troops shortly after D-Day. Each new issue contained extracts from BBC news broadcasts, messages from senior officers, notes on welfare and public relations, service humour and cartoons and odd items of griff picked up from German prisoners. This short extract from the news-sheet published at 12.00 hours on Wednesday, 14th June, referred to at least one German officer's reaction to the fighting at Bréville.

'An officer you captured from the GERMAN 346 Infantry Division complained that "it was *unfair* for troops of the sort found in 346 Infantry Division to be sent into action against BRITISH Airborne troops".'

The type-written copy in the news-sheets many times reveals the anxiety provoked by the doodle-bug raids on England, the monotony of compo stew and steak and veg and the friendly rivalry that existed between the red- and green-bereted troops. The Commandos' habit of digging deep – 'Monty says it will take twenty years to fill in their trenches' – caused the comment also that the Special Service Brigades had broken through to Australia. 'Nutty', the cartoonist, on one notable occasion went so far as to suggest that marsupials had been seen in the Commando lines!

The news-sheet was avidly read by the troops but its good humour belied the realities of the situation. Writing of the comparatively quiet period following Bréville, the unit historians of the 224th Parachute Field Ambulance, which was first set up under fire at Varaville on D-Day, have this to say:

'The slow attrition of mortar and mosquito wore down the men's morale. The mosquitoes, though not of course malarial, were voracious, multitudinous and venomous. They swarmed into the warm, dark trenches and bit through socks and even through battledress tunics. Next to the Germans, they were our greatest enemy.'

After the Battle of Bréville 6th Airborne Division stayed put in the green farmland and woods of Calvados with strict instructions from their news-sheet to 'keep off the cider-apples, please!' On 7th August General Gale received his instructions for the airborne's rôle in the pursuit to the Seine. The plan was for the Canadian First Army after marching on Falaise to swing south-east for the river near its estuary at Le Havre. The airborne division was to function as pivot of the Allied arm sweeping across France to the Seine. Gale was under orders to advance steadily eastwards but not to offer battle. There were two routes for him to pursue: a coastal road from Cabourg on the Dives to Trouville and Honfleur and a road from Troarn through Dozulé, Pont Leveque and Pont Audemer. The inevitable water barriers existed in the form of the Dives and its marshes, an adjacent canal and the Touques and Risle rivers. The distance from Cabourg to the Seine estuary at Honfleur is twelve miles.

The basis of General Gale's plan after clearing the west bank of the Dives was to send the Air-Landing, Belgian and Dutch Brigades along the northern route and to deploy the bulk of his forces from the area of Escoville through Bures and Troarn along the southern route. The code-name 'Paddle' seemed appropriate to the operation. Hill's 3rd Brigade led the attack at 03.00 hours on 17th August. Pearson's 8th Battalion was lead-ing when the brigade reached Bures before dawn. The battalion waded across the river while sappers set to work to replace the bridge blown up on D-Day. The sappers were indeed busy all the way to the Seine, building and repairing bridges, removing tree trunks from the roads and neutralising minefields. The 1st Canadian Parachute Battalion swept through the Bois de Bavent, in which the 8th had previously led a guerrilla-like existence, and crossed the Dives at four points. The 8th Battalion had reached Goustranville when after nightfall on the 18th the 9th Battalion (now Crookenden) passed through *en route* for Dozulé.

Thus began a leap-frog pattern of forward movements with 3rd and 5th Brigades alternating and each of their battalions taking it in turn to lead. Roaming German self-propelled guns and well-aimed mortar and machine-gun fire inflicted heavy casualties on the advancing troops. Poett's 5th Brigade and No 4 Commando passed over the Dives canal by a wooden bridge captured by the Canadians and renamed Canada Bridge. The approach to Dozulé was dominated by high ground concealing well-camouflaged defensive positions. The 13th Battalion seized Brucourt hill north of Dozulé but was thrown back; the 7th and 12th Battalions mean-while secured a firm base at Putot-en-Auge. Mills-Roberts' No 1 Com-mando succeeded where the 13th Battalion had failed and No 4 Commando took more high ground south of Putot-en-Auge; but Dozulé held firm until the Germans before withdrawing placed incendiaries in the houses and cottages and wantonly destroyed the town.

Dozulé was still burning when the 3rd Brigade overtaking the 5th Brigade struck out in the direction of Pont Leveque. The enclosed country-side was ideal for defensive tactics; a single self-propelled gun at a cross-roads was capable of holding up an entire battalion. Late on 21st August Poett's brigade now mounted in borrowed transport passed through again

<u>Pegasus Goes to It</u>

<u>1200 hours, Saturday, 5th August,1944.</u>   <u>No. 48.</u>

<u>An open letter to all who fight and work in the 6th AIRBORNE DIVISION.</u>

On the night of the 5th/6th August we shall have been in France for two months. During this time we have seen much, we have achieved much and we have all learned much. Most of us I think feel a little humble, for I am sure we must realize how much we all owe to the Almighty.

Many have left us wounded, some of them maimed for life: many have been killed: and many are still missing. These men were great comrades and we shall all miss them a very great deal. Those of us who are still here are grateful to them, and realize how much we owe to them.

I cannot for reasons of security publish now our figures of casualties; but I can assure you, beyond any question of dispute, that our losses are infinitely less than those we have inflicted on the enemy.

We have fought for ground and gained all we fought for: all we have gained by skill and guts we have held with courage and determination. Our reputation stands high in the 21st Army Group and at Home. Let us see to it that none of us lets the side down.

As I go about I am constantly struck by the smart and alert bearing of men in the red and green berets. Just as they look alert and businesslike in the line, so in the rear areas and across the river they look clean and soldierly and fit. There are exceptions, and it is up to you and me to see that those exceptions are eliminated. Do not let us get scruffy and untidy. In this division we all work to-gether; because we have a common interest and common ideal: it is that we should be second to none.

I frequently visit the cemetery where so many of our dead lie at rest. I hope you will do so when you can as well. There let each one of us re-dedicate himself to the cause which is ours.

I have had many letters from the bereaved ones at Home; for I write to them all; their courage and fortitude in the agony of their sorrow is great indeed. For their sakes, as well as for our own, let us lift up our heads in high resolve and pray to God that we shall be given strength to continue as we have commenced.

Go to it.

                         RICHARD N. GALE

In the Field,   Major General
5 August 1944.   6th Airborne Division

this time displaying an imposing array of guns and tanks. The Germans made a determined stand in the wide steep-sided Touques valley. Brigadier Poett instructed the 12th Battalion (now Stockwell) to occupy a dominating spur overlooking Pont Leveque called St Julien. North of the area No 4 Commando went for high ground controlling the Pont Leveque – Pont Audemer road. Meanwhile Luard's 13th Battalion was to cross the Touques at Pont Leveque and establish a bridgehead on the east bank.

Once inside the town of Pont Leveque, the airborne troops fought for every yard of ground. The 13th Battalion succeeded in crossing the river and Pine-Coffin's 7th Battalion was rushed up to hold the town. Hill's brigade with No 4 Commando still on the left were next in the line moving on to clear Beuzeville. Here the 8th Battalion spearheaded the capture of the town after a tough fight. The road from Beuzeville turns sharply south-eastwards to Pont Audemer on the Risle. Major-General Barker's 49th Division was routed to pass through this town to bridge the Seine, which lies less than five miles east of Pont Audemer. The Armoured Reconnaissance Regiment and the Dutch Brigade – transferred from the northern sector – arrived there first followed on foot by 7th Parachute Battalion. On 27th August 6th Airborne Division was ordered to stand down on a line from Honfleur on the coast to Pont Audemer.

The battle for the road from Cabourg to Honfleur was less strenuous but progress was impeded by mines and booby traps. The Belgian Brigade was responsible for bridging the Dives at Cabourg and after crossing the Touques the 1st RUR assisted by French Forces of the Interior pushed on to Beuville-sur-Mer. The Devons and the '52nd' – the traditional name of the Oxf. and Bucks – drove east on Branville, which was liberated to the sound of church bells on 22nd August. A recce platoon of the Devons clinging to the Touques municipal fire-engine entered Honfleur on the same day. By 30th August opposition west of the Seine had ceased.

Since 17th August the men of 6th Airborne Division, the two Commando brigades and their Belgian and Dutch comrades had covered thirty-five miles (as the crow flies) and liberated 400 square miles of France. In September after three months in the line, the division returned to its quarters on the Salisbury Plain. In its absence the English summer had gone by at Bulford and Netheravon. In Normandy, too, the landscape was changing colour but everywhere the autumn leaves chanced haphazardly upon the detritus of war. The airborne troops had left so many reminders of their own presence on the battlefield; dismembered gliders, the litter of abandoned equipment and the now deserted billets and medical posts. The total casualties suffered by 6th Airborne Division in Normandy numbered 4,557 all ranks; of this number 821 were killed in action, 2,709 seriously wounded and 927 posted as missing.

Operation 'Anvil'

Even as Allied troops swept victoriously across Normandy, another Allied force staged a second amphibious invasion, this time on the south coast of France between Cannes and Toulon. Behind a heavy air and naval bombardment three United States divisions (the 3rd, 36th and 45th), and an attached French armoured force began landing early on the morning of 15th August on either side of St Tropez. Meanwhile, a task force composed of American and British paratroopers landed behind the invasion beaches to cut roads and isolate the German defenders. The overall commander was Major-General Alexander M. Patch, commander of the United States Seventh Army. 1st Airborne Task Force, which was led by Major-General R. T. Frederick, US Army, consisted of five US parachute battalions, one US air-landing brigade and Pritchard's 2nd British Independent Parachute Brigade Group. The fly-in from Rome of the parachutists was handled by 51 US Troop Carrier Wing; a glider force numbering sixty-one Wacos and Horsas followed on with the support weapons.

The 2nd Brigade's task on Operation 'Anvil', which has been described as the 'Champagne' invasion, was to capture the road junction village of Le Muy some fifteen miles inland from Fréjus. The Pathfinders went in first at 03.20 hours to plant 'Eureka' beacons but the drop from 125 aircraft was very scattered. The 4th and 6th Parachute Battalions assembled at first light at about half strength on the DZ but the 5th was distributed across about twenty miles of French territory. The glider landings were successfully completed in two stages during the day. The 6th (Royal Welch) Battalion captured Le Muy and by nightfall on the 15th the 2nd Brigade was in control of all three roads into the village. The British paratroopers made good friends with the Maquis and were withdrawn after suffering only slight casualties on 26th August to Italy.

Horsa glider on tow.

5. Military Operations – A Bridge too Far!

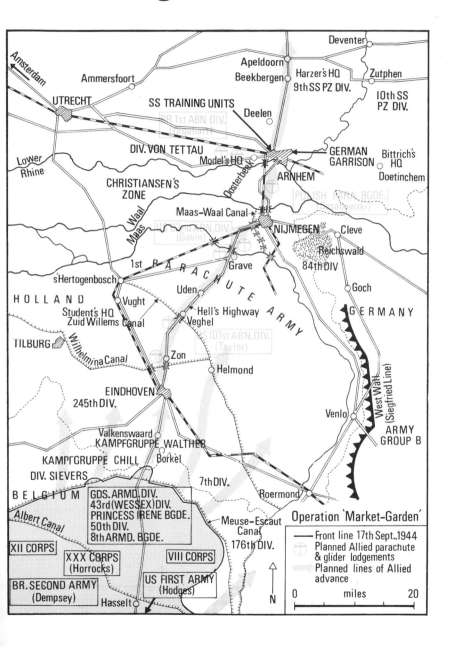

Operation 'Market-Garden': the objectives, line of advance of the Second Army and dispositions of the German forces.

Operation 'Market-Garden'

General Montgomery's reasons for launching Operation 'Market-Garden' on 17th September 1944 and for employing 1st Airborne at Arnhem have already been stated. Major-General Roy E. Urquhart had seven days in which to organise his rôle in 'Market', the code-name for the Anglo-US contribution to 'Garden', the Second Army offensive from the Meuse-Escaut line. Although Urquhart was new to airborne forces he was already a veteran airborne planner. Of the sixteen or so divisional plans produced since D-Day most had reached the flight manifest and loading stages before last-minute cancellation. Amongst these various schemes 'Wild Oats', for example, was aimed at St Malo; 'Hands Up' meant the Germans at Vannes and 'Transfigure' was intended as an Anglo-US airborne bid for Paris. Operation 'Comet' cancelled on 10th September involved 1st Airborne Division in capturing *all three* of the Maas, Waal and Rhine crossings. Consequently the divisional commander and his staff already had some knowledge of the geography of Arnhem when they sat down to plan Operation 'Market'.

Prior to the war few outside Holland had ever heard of Arnhem. For foreign travellers conveyed by rail from the Hook of Holland via Utrecht to Cologne, the Neder Rijn is first observed a few miles west of Arnhem. Pre-war tourists may have noted from their *Blue Guides* at this point that Arnhem was a town of some 80,000 inhabitants; the Grand Hotel du Soleil charged no more than $6\frac{1}{2}$–$8\frac{1}{2}$ florins a day for full board; the Hotel de Tafelberg at nearby Oosterbeek costing less at 6–8 florins a day. Arnhem apparently displayed a fine Gothic church called *Groote Kerk* and a large expanse of parkland known as *Park Sonsbeek*; electric trams in 1939 were gradually replacing steam trams; and the more adventurous Rhine steamers alternated a daily service to Rotterdam and Mannheim. Arnhem, the capital of Guelderland, was said to be a favourite spot for retired 'nabobs' from the East Indies.

At the Hotel de Tafelberg in Oosterbeek in September 1944 *Generalfeldmarschall* Walter Model had no immediate worries about an airborne landing to seize the Arnhem road bridge. As commander-in-chief in the West and also local commander of Army Group B, he considered that Allied airborne intervention in Holland was imminent but that Eindhoven was the most likely location for parachute and glider landings. In Model's opinion Montgomery was a prudent commander and the former was certain that Nijmegen and Arnhem were too far from the Allied line for the latter to contemplate airborne intervention. The German field-marshal was more concerned with blocking the onward path of Dempsey's Second Army assembling on the Dutch frontier. The German opposition to XXX Corps between Eindhoven and Nijmegen along the proposed line of advance to Arnhem, Apeldoorn and the Zuider Zee was formed by *Generaloberst* Kurt Student's First Parachute Army. Kurt Student, whose headquarters was at Vught, commanded a group comprising some veteran *Fallschirmjäger* units but rather more infantry and armoured units.

Student's operational zone lay well to the south of Arnhem. The quality of the resistance to XXX Corps was more the concern of Lieutenant-General Brian Horrocks, but it was upon his success in driving sixty miles from the frontier straight through First Parachute Army that Urqu-

General Sir Miles Dempsey, British Second Army.

Major-General R. E. Urquhart, GOC 1st Airborne Division.

Major-General Stanislaw Sosabowski, 1st Polish Independent Parachute Brigade Group.

hart depended for survival. (Gavin's US 82nd Airborne at Nijmegen relied no less on timely relief but an early link-up seemed assured for Taylor's US 101st Airborne north of Eindhoven.) Enemy forces north of the Waal were thought to be thin on the ground. Intelligence sources accurately reported the existence of about 2,000 SS recruits in the Arnhem area itself, a heavy concentration of anti-aircraft batteries near the road bridge and Luftwaffe personnel at Deelen airfield seven miles north of Arnhem. *Generalleutnant* Hans von Tettau's division west of Arnhem in fact consisted of small units spread out on a line forty miles wide. Close to Arnhem was an SS NCOs school under *Oberst* Lippert and an SS Panzer Grenadier training and depot battalion (Bn 16) under SS *Sturmbannführer* Sepp Krafft.

General Jim Gavin, 82nd Airborne Division.

British intelligence assessments did not take into serious account the existence also near Arnhem of Willi Bittrich's II Panzer Corps. SS *Obergruppenführer und General der Waffen-SS* Wilhelm Bittrich's 9th and 10th SS Panzer Divisions were on 3rd September ordered to rest and refit north and east of Arnhem on the Veluwe and in the Achterhoek. Both divisions, which were nearly wiped out at Caen and Falaise, now limped like two wounded lions via Cambrai and Mons across Belgium into Holland. Although Dutch agents signalled the arrival of these battered divisions in the neighbourhood of Arnhem, British senior officers simply did not believe that they were strong enough to offer battle. Harzer's 9th SS (Hohenstaufen) Division was stationed west of the Yssel with its headquarters at Beekbergen twelve miles north of Arnhem. Harmel's 10th SS (Frundsberg) Division with its headquarters at Ruurlo near Zutphen was situated east of the Yssel. Willi Bittrich's HQ was located fifteen miles due east of Arnhem at Doetinchem.

General Maxwell D. Taylor, 101st Airborne Division.

1,543 parachute and tug aircraft were available to Browning's 1st Airborne Corps. The British share of 519 aircraft was equitable but insufficient to transport three British and one Polish brigade to Arnhem in one single airborne operation. This meant that as on 6th June in Normandy the airborne troops would again be denied the tactical benefits of rapid concentration in strength. In addition all those going in after the first lift were exposed to the certain danger of landing in the face of an alerted enemy. The British allotment of aircraft was made up of 279 Dakota C-47s and 240 RAF converted bombers. Most of the latter were Stirlings but there were forty Halifaxes and also a few Albemarles. The US 9th Troop Carrier Command laid on the Dakotas for the parachutists and sixteen squadrons of Nos 38 and 46 Groups RAF were responsible for the glider element.

The Arnhem countryside is an area of woods, heathland, villages and country estates. No attempt was to be made to land an assault party at the bridge as the polderland bordering on the river was considered unsuitable for the landing of glider or parachute troops. The Royal Air Force in turn objected to flying too close to the bridge because of the flak batteries. In the circumstances General Urquhart had no alternative but to select his main landing area north of the river in open country flanked by woods six miles west of Arnhem. Three daylight lifts on 17th, 18th and 19th September were planned as follows:

General Walter Harzer, 9th SS Panzer (Hohenstaufen) Division.

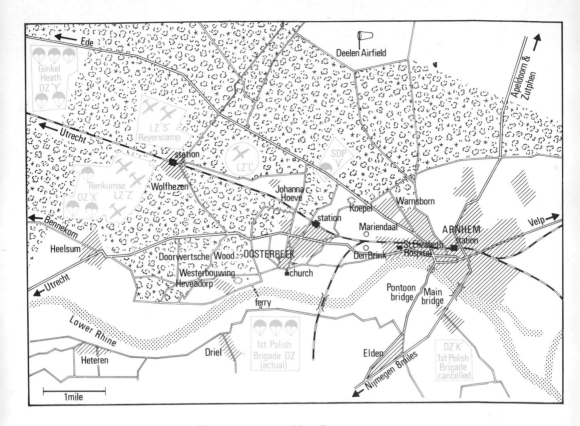

Arnhem. The dropping and landing zones.

SUNDAY 17th SEPTEMBER. *1st Parachute Brigade* (Lathbury) was
assigned to seize the Arnhem bridge and a pontoon bridge further west.
The brigade preceded by the 21st Independent Parachute Company was to
drop on DZ 'X' near Heelsum on the south side of the Utrecht-Arnhem
railway line. Brigadier Lathbury's long-term objective was to hold the
north and south banks of the river on the eastern side of the southern
entrance to Arnhem. This area to the north of the river embraced the
commercial centre of the town. 157 Dakotas were needed to drop the
brigade as well as recce troops, gunners, sappers, medics and elements of
Div. HQ. *1st (Air-Landing) Brigade* (Hicks) was to fly in at the same
time and land on LZ 'Z'. 345 Horsas and thirteen Hamilcars were allotted
to carry the air-landing battalions and more support and service troops
along with a mass of equipment. 'X' and 'Z' were adjacent territories and
represented virtually the only treeless country west of Arnhem between the
river and the railway line. The glider brigade's job was firstly to secure the
landing areas for the following day and then to occupy similar positions to
1st Parachute Brigade on both banks of the river on the west side of the
road. This lodgement area extended westwards from Arnhem about a mile
beyond Oosterbeek. The Armoured Reconnaissance Squadron was to
make the initial assault on the Arnhem bridge.

MONDAY 18th SEPTEMBER. *4th Parachute Brigade* (Hackett) with
gunners, sappers and medics also under command was to drop from 124

114

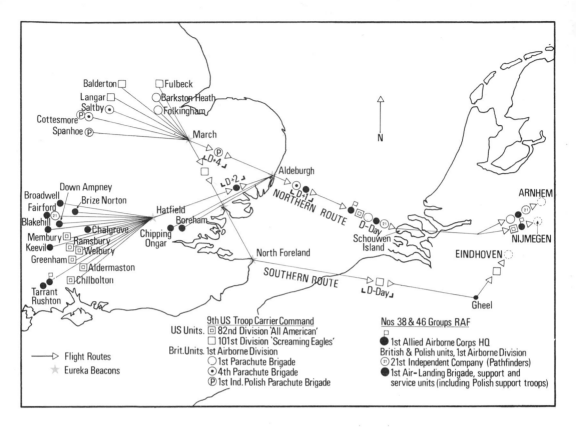

Operation 'Market'. The emplaning airfields in the United Kingdom and the air route plan to Eindhoven, Nijmegen and Arnhem.

Dakotas on DZ 'Y' 2,000 yards north-west of 'X' and 'Z' on the far side of the railway line. LZ 'S' to the east of DZ 'Y' was to receive 286 Horsas and fifteen Hamilcars bearing the remainder of the 1st (Air-Landing) Brigade and the Royal Artillery. Another zone ('L') near Wolfhezen was designated as a re-supply area for a drop by thirty-five Stirlings. Brigadier Hackett's orders were to occupy the high ground north of Arnhem. The terrain north of the railway line as to the south with the exception of those areas chosen for the landings is covered in woodland.

TUESDAY 19th SEPTEMBER. *1st Polish Independent Parachute Brigade Group* (Sosabowski) was on call with the original intention of jumping from 114 Dakotas on DZ 'K' one mile to the south of the bridge. Major-General Stanislaw Sosabowski's brief was to assist in the capture of the bridge if necessary and then to pass through 1st Parachute Brigade to hold ground north-east of the town. The Polish brigade would thus complete the divisional jigsaw pattern of defences in and around the Arnhem area. Forty-five tug aircraft would at the same time as the brigade drop bring in more Polish troops and US Aviation engineers on the re-supply zone 'L' of the previous day. 163 RAF aircraft were also scheduled to make a major re-supply drop as part of the third lift. This was to be on SDP 'V' at Warnsborn on the outskirts of Arnhem.

On the morning of 17th September the first lift took off for Holland from twenty-four RAF and USTCC bases in East Anglia and Southern England. Overland fog prevailed in the early morning but soon cleared and the first aircraft took off in favourable weather at 10.25 hours. The whole of the first lift was airborne within ninety minutes. The two carrier fleets were protected by 371 Tempests, Spitfires and Mosquitoes and 548 Thunderbolts, Mustangs and Lightnings. During the night the RAF attacked airfields in Holland and in the morning 139 Lancasters and twenty Mosquitoes flew in two waves to work over flak positions. Then 816 Flying Fortresses, escorted by 161 Mustangs and 212 P-47s, bombed 117 coastal flak and inland batteries. The result of this magnificent support was that the losses in carrier aircraft were slight.

Prior to take-off the senior officers of 1st Airborne Division were supremely confident of success and after the frustration of so many cancelled orders even jubilant at the prospect of battle. Success in Operation 'Market-Garden' must surely mean the downfall of the Third Reich before Christmas. Miles Dempsey was one of the few British generals who really understood the airborne method and Monty had promised on his behalf that units of the Second Army would be in Arnhem on D-Day plus two. At the briefing the airborne officers had perhaps been too eager to accept the intelligence assessments of the enemy opposition in the Arnhem area. At the previous briefing for Operation 'Comet' only the sometimes obdurate but always courageous Sosabowski had questioned the almost carefree mood of optimism. After Urquhart had outlined his plan, Sosabowski leapt to his feet and shouted: 'But the *Germans*, General, the *Germans*!'

After the 'fat-free' cookhouse breakfasts for the men, the NAAFI and 'Sally Anne' waggons at the emplaning airfields did a brisk business in hot tea and wads. The men in a mood perhaps of semi-tension lay back on the grass resting on their parachute packs. After the fog cleared the sun was warm and the weight of their clothing and equipment made life warmer still. The flight across the North Sea was almost uneventful. When a few aircraft went down with engine trouble and some of the glider towropes snapped, Air-Sea Rescue launches stationed in a chain across the water moved out of line to pick up survivors. After the aircraft crossed the yellow sand dunes and brown scrub of Schouwen, it was Sunday, too, in Holland and there was no sign of war in the peaceful countryside.

'Boy' Browning travelled to his Corps HQ location near Nijmegen in a Horsa glider piloted by Brigadier George Chatterton. For the immaculate general dressed in a barathea battledress with knife-edge creases, and a gleaming Sam Browne belt and revolver holster, 'Market-Garden' was the crowning moment of his military career. But his own optimism was restrained reflectively by a note of caution. On the same morning in Belgium Brian Horrocks was standing on a slag heap by the Meuse Escaut Canal with his field glasses trained northward for the first sight of the airborne armada. As soon as 1st Airborne Corps touched down his orders would send the Guards Armoured Division thundering down the road to Eindhoven. Some 20,000 Corps vehicles were waiting for Horrocks' signal to move. 'We can hold the Arnhem bridge for four days,' Browning had said, 'but I think we might be going a bridge too far.'

Stick waiting to emplane.

The flight to Holland. Inside a Dakota.

Order of Battle
1st Airborne Division: Operation 'Market'
The Battle of Arnhem — 17th–26th September 1944

General Officer Commanding
MAJOR-GENERAL R. E. URQUHART DSO

Div. HQ

CRA *Loder-Symonds*
CRE *Myers*
Div. Signals *Stephenson*
CRASC *St J. Packe*
ADMS *Warrack*
ADOS *Mobbs*
Adj. REME *Ewens*
SCF *Harlow*
Prov. *Haig*

4th Parachute Brigade
BRIG. J. W. HACKETT DSO, MBE, MC

156th Para. Bn *de B. des Voeux*
10th Para. Bn *Smyth*
11th Para. Bn *Lea*

2 A/L Lt Bty RA *Linton*
2 A/L A-Tk Bty RA *Haynes*
4 Para. Sqn RE *Perkins*
133 Para. Fd Amb. *Alford*

Div. Troops

1st Light Regt RA *Thompson*
No 1 FOU
9 Fd Coy RE
21 Indep. Para. Coy
250 Lt Coy RASC
93 Coy RASC (det.)
Ord. Fd PKS (det.)
REME Wksps (det.)
89 Fd Security Sec.
Div. Prov. Coy
No 1 Wing GP Regt *Murray*
No 2 Wing GP Regt *Place*

1st Parachute Brigade
BRIG. G. W. LATHBURY DSO, MBE

Recce Sqn *Gough*
(less one troop)

1st Para. Bn *Dobie*
2nd Para. Bn *Frost*
3rd Para. Bn *Fitch*

3 A/L Bty RA *Mumford*
1 A/L A-Tk Bty RA *Arnold*
1 Para. Sqn RE *Murray*
16 Para. Fd Amb. *Townsend*

1st Air-Landing Brigade
BRIG. P. H. W. HICKS DSO, MC

1st Bn Border *Hadden*
7th Bn KOSB *Payton-Reid*
2nd Bn South Staffs. *McCardie*

1 A/L Lt Bty RA *Norman Walker*
181 Para. Fd Amb. *Marrable*

SEABORNE TAIL
(vehicles and equipment)

OC *Sellon*
Div. HQ. 1 Para. Bgde. 4 Para Bgde
A/L Bgde. Recce Sqn. RASC. Lt Regt

The 21st Independent Parachute Company dropping through the holes of twelve Stirling aircraft landed precisely at mid-day to slight opposition from small arms fire. Major B. A. Wilson's Pathfinders numbering six officers and 186 men had acquired a German staff car and sixteen prisoners before they heard the deep throb of the approaching aircraft. The tug bombers towing the gliders came first followed by the carrier aircraft. The glider and parachute landings occurring between 13.15 and 14.00 hours were the most successful that had been achieved by either side during the war. The glider pilots handling their flimsy craft with considerable skill came in on the Pathfinders' smoke signals and orange and crimson

Arnhem. The first
lift arrives.

Gliders on the
ground. Some landed
in the trees. The skid
marks can be plainly
seen.

LZ 'Z'. The first two gliders to land. An HQ RA party about to move off.

nylon markers with tremendous accuracy. On touch-down the ground was grazed by skid marks as the gliders slithered to a standstill. Punctually on time came the Dakotas and the blue sky blossomed with over 2,000 parachutes of many colours floating gently to earth in the warm breeze.

Although no gliders were actually shot down *en route* thirty-five of them failed to make the LZ and this unfortunately meant the loss of the reconnaissance squadron's armoured jeeps. Major C. F. H. ('Freddie') Gough's recce troops were accordingly re-assigned from their original objective of seizing the bridge and Frost's 2nd Parachute Battalion was ordered to lead the way. The battalion forming single files on either side of the road advanced into Heelsum and through the Doorwertsche Wood along the north bank of the river towards the town. The 3rd Battalion (Fitch) set off also on foot along the main Utrecht-Arnhem road from Heelsum to Oosterbeek intending to approach Arnhem from the north. Gerald Lathbury's Brigade HQ followed slowly in jeeps in the wake of Frost's battalion on the southern road. The 1st Battalion (Dobie) was in reserve with instructions to approach Arnhem north of Fitch's route in the centre via Wolfhezen station to the Ede-Arnhem road. As the brigade advanced past red-tiled cottages and wealthy villas, Dutch civilians in their Sunday attire waved enthusiastically. Many of them were wearing Orange emblems.

Meanwhile, the majority of the glider troops moved across the railway line to take up their defensive positions for the arrival of the second lift

on the following day. At roll call, the 7th Bn the King's Own Scottish Borderers (Payton-Reid) having lost eight gliders in transit showed a total of 740, all ranks, of whom forty were officers. Pipers playing 'Blue Bonnets' rallied the men to their companies and by 15.00 hours they were ready to move off to occupy positions surrounding DZ 'Y' at Ginkel Heath. Arnhem was the 7th KOSB's first and last action·in the war; the parade strength ten days later numbered only four officers and seventy-two men. McCardie's 2nd South Staffords dug in to the east of the Scotsmen around the perimeter of LZ 'S' near Reyerscamp; Hadden's 1st Bn the Border Regiment also successfully occupied their allotted area south of the railway line at Renkum Heath.

1st Parachute Brigade on the afternoon of the 17th was already experiencing a foretaste of things to come. John Frost, whose exploits since Bruneval had added the DSO to his MC, led his battalion through Heelsum ambushing German vehicles and taking prisoners before encountering opposition in the Doorwertsche wood. Further along the road 'B' Company was detached to subdue machine-gunners on the high ground called Den Brink and then to capture the pontoon bridge which was officially listed as the brigade's secondary target. This bridge was still undamaged but the Germans had removed some of the barges and towed them to a nearby river dock. Frost now ran into a problem that was already perplexing the divisional commander; the wireless sets would not

The Arnhem bridge. This aerial photograph was taken on the second day of the battle. The buildings on the left and right of the road on the north bank of the Lower Rhine were the scene of the epic stand by 2nd Parachute Battalion.

Generaloberst Kurt Student.

work and inter-unit communication except by means of runner was impossible.

At dusk 'A' Company was inside Arnhem and observing military and civilian traffic crossing the road bridge. In an attempt to cross the bridge from the north Lieutenant Grayburn and his platoon met with a hail of fire from two quick firing, 20-mm flak guns, and from the machine-guns of an armoured car. Although shot through the arm Grayburn organised the withdrawal of his men to a house that was vital to the defence of the bridge. When Frost arrived he established his HQ in a house north-west of the bridge in a street known as Ne Kraan. The bridge was completely intact but was soon under mortar attack. The battalion commander sent word to 'B' Company to cross the river in boats and secure the southern end of the bridge but these men were still fighting a sharp engagement at Den Brink. No news came from 'C' Company most of whom were under attack back at the railway bridge. Nevertheless, the force in Arnhem increased during the night; elements of Fitch's 3rd Battalion and part of Brigade HQ arrived but without Brigadier Lathbury. In the morning the number of parachutists at the bridge totalled some 600–700 men.

The main body of the 3rd Battalion had been brought to a standstill west of Oosterbeek. Here the paratroopers were halted by mortar fire from Krafft's battalion but when it was discovered that enemy tanks were on the road Lathbury ordered Fitch to dig in by the roadside. The information that the armour belonged to the 9th SS (Hohenstaufen) Division came as a shattering blow. Caution now mingled with doubt as to the accuracy of the intelligence estimates of enemy strengths. Before reaching the Ede-Arnhem road, the CO of the 1st Battalion was informed by Major Freddie Gough that this road was also blocked by armour and that Panzer Grenadier troops were distributed along the railway line from Wolfhezen into Arnhem. During the first night Dobie's battalion was entrenched on the edge of a line of woods east of Wolfhezen station.

The timing of the airborne landings west of Oosterbeek commencing at 13.15 hours (British Summer Time) registered as one hour earlier local time. Field-Marshal Model, who right then was enjoying a pre-luncheon drink at the Tafelberg, immediately abandoned his headquarters and motored to Arnhem to see the commander of the town garrison, General Kussin. Thence Model took the road east to Doetinchem to the headquarters of Willi Bittrich, the commander of II Panzer Corps. If Model had remained a few hours longer in Oosterbeek, he would have received the full details of Operation 'Market-Garden' over the telephone that afternoon from Kurt Student in Vught. Student had seen the American air fleet flying north to Eindhoven from their turning point on the diversionary course across Belgium. An American glider hit by flak had crashed close to his HQ killing both passengers and crew. A document file taken from a dead officer's kit revealed all the unit strengths and objectives of 1st Airborne Corps and by mid-afternoon these important papers were lying on Student's desk.

It is ironic of course that it should have been Student who was studying those plans that day in Holland. In 1941 four months after the German airborne invasion of Crete, Hitler had informed Student that the inherent risks in airborne warfare were too great to ever consider such an operation again. When the father of the *Fallschirmjäger* and pioneer of the airborne method saw the fly-past at Vught, his sense of frustration was understandable. 'Oh, how I wish,' he cried to his chief-of-staff, 'that I had ever had such powerful means at my disposal!'

Even though on Sunday, 17th September, Model and Bittrich had not so far had the opportunity of studying the captured dossier, it was not so very difficult – with the news also of the American landing at Nijmegen – for them to assess the Allied objectives on the Maas, Waal and Lower Rhine. Kussin was instructed by Model to inform Hitler; Hans Albin Rauter, *SS Reichskommissar* for Holland, was in turn told to alert Himmler. The elderly Hans von Tettau – allegedly awe-stricken by what he had seen of the fly-in – was ordered to send all his available units to assist the Lippert and Krafft battalions west of Arnhem. Bittrich had already issued orders to his two SS Panzer divisions. Model concurred with Bittrich's initiative.

'*9th SS Panzer* (*Hohenstaufen*) *Division*
    1. Division to reconnoitre in the direction of Arnhem and Nijmegen.
    2. The division to go immediately into action occupying the Arnhem area and destroying the enemy forces which have landed to the west of Arnhem at Oosterbeek. Immediate attack is essential. The aim is to occupy and firmly hold the bridge at Arnhem.

'*10th SS Panzer* (*Frundsberg*) *Division*
    Division to proceed immediately to Nijmegen, occupying the main bridge in strength, and defending the bridge-heads.'

At midday on the 17th *Gruppenführer* Harzer of the Hohenstaufen Division was driving from Beekbergen to his reconnaissance battalion's location to present the Iron Cross to one of his officers. Harzer actually received Bittrich's orders at 13.30 hours and the former moved quickly to his tasks. The immediate importance of the Arnhem road bridge to Bittrich

1st Parachute Battalion in action in Oosterbeek.

1 3-inch mortar team.

2 Vickers machine-gun in action.

3 Signallers waiting to repulse an attack.

4 On the outskirts of Arnhem. Piat gunner and rifleman; Bren gunner on the far side of the road.

1

2

3

4

was that it would enable Harmel's Frundsberg and elements of the Hohenstaufen Divisions to cross quickly over the Lower Rhine to Nijmegen. Although the Hohenstaufen Division, which was to oppose 1st Airborne Division from the east was well below strength its superiority in fire power was immense. The Panzers possessed armoured cars, 43-ton Panzer tanks, the heavier Tiger tanks, self-propelled guns and well-seasoned infantry carried in half-track vehicles and lorries.

At 1st Airborne Div HQ, which on the first afternoon was set up on the edge of the glider LZ, General Urquhart found the going tough from the start. While the German commanders were briskly mobilising their units over the public telephone system, the airborne signallers in the closely-wooded, sandy terrain were having little or no luck with their radio sets. Contact was soon lost with 1st Parachute Brigade moving along the approach roads to Arnhem; W/T communications with base in the United Kingdom were weak and erratic. No contact was raised direct with Corps HQ at Nijmegen but messages could be sent using the UK base as a rear link. Urquhart, who knew nothing of Frost's success in reaching the bridge, resolved to find out what was going on. The general set off at the wheel of a jeep with a signaller on the back seat and presently caught up with rear elements of the 2nd Battalion. On the morning of the 18th he was with Gerald Lathbury, who had attached himself to the 3rd Battalion on the Utrecht-Arnhem road General Kussin, who had earlier been driven out from Arnhem to reconnoitre this road, lay dead by the roadside killed by a burst from a Bren gun.

Moving in files into Arnhem.

125

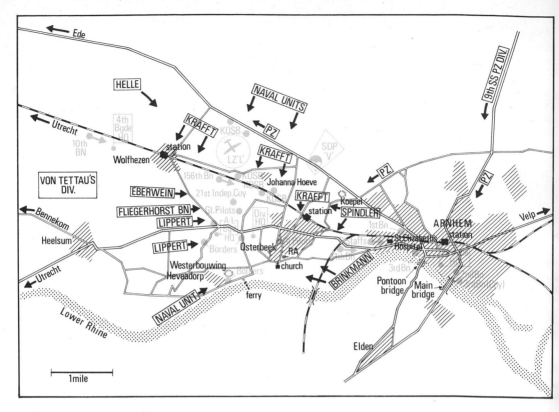

Unit locations of 1st Airborne Division and the enemy opposition on 18th September.

Fitch's 3rd Battalion was practically surrounded and the road was being mortared but patrols pressed on into Arnhem. Urquhart now had no choice but to stay with Lathbury and later in the day Brigade HQ succeeded in passing through the outskirts of Arnhem to occupy a villa inside the town. By now Frost's force strengthened by Gough's squadron was still lodged at the northern end of the bridge in groups of houses and warehouses. Attacks by armoured cars and Panzer Grenadiers dismounting from half-track vehicles were repulsed with grenades, an anti-tank gun and Piats. Frost repeatedly directed machine-gun fire across the bridge to prevent the enemy from forming at the southern end but this only attracted more and more shells and mortar bombs and by evening the whole battalion area was a blazing inferno. The streets were strewn with the wreckage of tram cars, buses and motor cars and the people of Arnhem, who had openly welcomed the paratroopers, now sensibly took to their cellars. At the St Elizabeth Hospital in Arnhem 16th (Parachute) Field Ambulance, which had moved forward from the DZ with Brigade HQ, was fully operational with the help of Dutch doctors and nurses on the Sunday evening. On the following day SS troops took over the hospital but allowed the two surgical teams to carry on with their work.

Lieutenant Grayburn, the officer who was wounded in the initial assault on the bridge, and his platoon occupied a house that was vital to its defence. The house, which was outside the main defensive perimeter, was exposed and difficult to defend and the enemy ceaselessly attacked the position, using infantry supported by mortars and machine-guns. The platoon resisted all these attacks for two days and on the 20th Grayburn organised fighting patrols to stop the enemy from entering neighbouring houses. This forced the Germans to bring up tanks and self-propelled guns and the house came under such heavy fire that the platoon was obliged to retire to an area further north. German engineers now attempted to lay demolition charges at the bridge; Grayburn led a fighting patrol, which drove the enemy off temporarily, and gave time for the fuses to be removed. He was again wounded, this time in the back, but refused to be evacuated. Finally, an enemy tank, against which the paratroopers had no defence, approached so close to Grayburn's new position in the town that it became untenable. He stood up in full view of the tank and directed his men to the main defensive perimeter. Lieutenant John Grayburn, 2nd Bn the Parachute Regiment, who was posthumously awarded the Victoria Cross for 'supreme courage, leadership and devotion to duty', was killed that night by a flame-thrower.

In England on the morning of the 18th the take-off of the second lift due at Arnhem at 10.00 hours had been delayed by fog and it was 15.00 hours before the landings commenced. The glider pilots again performed magnificently and the Dakota pilots pin-pointed the DZ at Ginkel Heath with great accuracy. Both the 7th KOSB and 2nd South Staffords had been in action since early morning and the woodland abutting the reception zones was ablaze. 4th Parachute Brigade flew in at 500 feet through flak bursts and the parachutists on descending heard the crack of rifle fire and the thud of mortar bombs exploding on the ground. A fairly strong wind was blowing and some of the men dropped into the fir trees. Payton-Reid ordered the 7th KOSB to fix bayonets and he led a vigorous charge to clear the woods, fields and ditches of Germans aiming rifle bullets at the aircraft. One Dakota hit by flak burst into flames over the DZ but the paratroopers jumped clear before the aircraft plunged helplessly to the ground.

Brigadier J. W. 'Shan' Hackett hit the ground only 200 yards from his first location for Brigade HQ. A brief search in the heather failed to reveal his walking-stick, which had parted company with him on the way down. After recovering from this minor setback, Hackett's alert mind quickly deduced that all was not well. The divisional commander had been swallowed up in a maze of streets in Arnhem and news from 1st Parachute Brigade was scarce. Before Hackett's arrival, Brigadier 'Pip' Hicks had reluctantly moved over from 1st (Air-Landing) Brigade HQ to assume command of the division. (Lathbury was actually Urquhart's senior brigadier but as he was also missing Hicks was next in the chain of command.) Hicks had no reason to change the divisional plan and his first concern was to strengthen the 1st and 3rd Battalions' endeavours to reinforce Frost at the bridge. McCardie's South Staffords (some of whom had flown in on the second lift) were ordered forward from Reyerscamp with all speed to the town. As further reinforcement Lea's 11th Parachute Battalion was detached from 4th Brigade on the DZ and instructed to march in the rear of the glider battalion.

The Battle of Arnhem was now assuming a definite pattern. Frost's besieged battalion group was engaged in a desperate struggle with Panzer forces at the bridge. Four battalions, the 1st, 3rd, the South Staffords and the 11th, were fighting their way, yard by yard, into the town. It will be remembered that the 1st and 3rd Battalions had been forced to dig in not long after leaving their DZ on the Sunday evening. When Dobie and Fitch resumed the advance on the following morning, both battalions moved south to infiltrate the solid wall of armour. Although lacerated by machine-gun fire and mortar bombs, Dobie and Fitch succeeded in breaking into the town but whereas Dobie met up later with McCardie and Lea in Arnhem, Fitch was at first unaware of the presence of the other three battalions operating in the same area of the St Elizabeth Hospital. Fitch immediately led the 3rd Battalion in an attack mounted at 16.00 hours on the 18th via the railway line towards the bridge.

Later the same day Hackett's 4th Brigade with the 156th Battalion leading the 10th Battalion was moving along the line of the railway towards Johanna Hoeve east of Wolfhezen. This route ran past the Reyerscamp LZ where the 4th Brigade picked up their transport and equipment. The 7th KOSB after completing their guard duties at Ginkel Heath were proceeding on the left flank to secure zone 'L' for the Polish glider landing twenty-four hours later. 1st Borders after a mauling at Renkum Heath were advancing south of the railway line in the direction of their allotted posts in the Arnhem perimeter. These four battalions were supported in their advance by Thompson's three 75-mm batteries, the glider pilots turned foot soldiers and other div units. At dawn on the 19th Hackett decided to form a Brigade base line with Kenneth Smyth's 10th Battalion at Johanna Hoeve and to send Sir Richard de B. des Voeux's 156th Battalion forward to capture the village of Koepel on the high ground north of Arnhem. But the movement of the main body of troops into Arnhem was already doomed. An iron chain was rapidly closing around the four square miles of airborne territory north of Oosterbeek.

Kampfgruppe Harzer acting promptly on Bittrich's orders first arrived in Arnhem on the evening of the 17th and then split up into two sub-groups. Brinkmann's group was ordered to patrol the town with armour and infantry and to clear the houses of British parachutists. Spindler's *Sperrgruppe* (blocking-group) was assigned to creating a wall of armour and infantry on the outskirts of Arnhem and to patrol forward along the three 'approach' routes into the town. In the centre Lippert and Krafft's battalions *in situ* were offering strong resistance with machine-gun, mortar and sniper fire and more of von Tettau's units were moving in from the north and west. To the south lay the river but Brinkmann's troops were edging along the north bank.

The 156th Battalion attacked strongly but was repulsed with heavy losses. The 10th Battalion was driven back before reaching Johanna Hoeve and forced to dig in alongside the Utrecht-Arnhem road. Smyth's 'Sussex' Battalion remained under devastating fire from flak guns, SPs, tanks and mortars throughout the day. During this bitter onslaught on the 19th, Captain Lionel Queripel, who was posthumously awarded the Victoria Cross for his bravery, was acting as company commander of a composite company of men from three battalions. In the afternoon his company was advancing down a main road leading to the north bank of the river when machine-gun fire drove the men to cover on both sides of the road.

Captain Queripel, who had served with the 10th Battalion since Kabrit days, crossed and recrossed the road under fire to reorganise his force. After carrying a wounded sergeant to the Regimental Aid Post, he led an attack on a strongpoint killing the crews of two machine-guns and of a captured British anti-tank gun. Later Queripel, who was wounded in the face, found himself cut off with a small party of men and took up a position in a ditch. Although wounded again he continued to inspire his men to return heavy mortar and Spandau fire with grenades, pistols and a few remaining rifles. On one occasion he picked up an unexploded stick grenade and threw it back at the enemy. As, however, the enemy pressure increased, so Captain Queripel decided to order his men to withdraw. Despite their protests, he insisted on remaining behind to cover their withdrawal with his automatic pistol and a few hand grenades. This was the last occasion on which he was seen alive.

Captain L. E. Queripel VC, 10th Parachute Battalion.

Inside Arnhem, Frost's force was still clinging desperately to the north-west end of the bridge. No more attempts were made to capture the southern end. The original force at the bridge comprised 'A' and 'C' Company (2nd Bn), 'C' Company (3rd Bn), 1st Parachute Brigade HQ, elements of the Recce Squadron and a few anti-tank gunners, engineers and RASC personnel. These men were actually spread out in about forty houses and other buildings including a school. The whole of Arnhem was burning fiercely and Tiger tanks rumbled through the streets shelling each suspected hiding place. Frost himself was badly wounded in the leg and Major Freddie Gough assumed command. Gough and those still un-wounded (their hopes raised by rumours that a breakthrough by the 1st and 3rd Battalions was imminent) continued to offer resistance. Some minor successes were registered against the tanks with a handful of anti-tank guns and Piat bombs. But conditions grew worse and worse until finally the only means of moving under cover was by blowing holes in the dividing walls of the houses. At dusk on the 20th the Germans were moving in on the last remaining strongholds with flame-throwers.

The story of the Battle of Arnhem is often only associated with the defence of the bridge but for courage and self-sacrifice the drive on the 19th from the St Elizabeth Hospital to relieve Frost's isolated troops has seldom been emulated in military history. As we have learned Fitch with the 3rd Battalion set off in Frost's direction immediately on arrival in Arnhem. The advance commenced from the railway marshalling yards north of the hospital but the battalion was enfiladed from high ground on both sides by machine-guns and mortars on the left and by artillery to the south of the river. The 3rd Battalion was split in half by the continuous fire and Fitch ordered his men to fall back under the cover of darkness to the Rhine Pavilion on the embankment. Dobie, McCardie and Lea were then planning their assault through the network of streets lying between the railway line and the river. The advance was to begin from a north-south line extending from the St Elizabeth Hospital to the Rhine Pavilion. The South Staffords, who had been reinforced by their men from the second lift, followed by the 11th Battalion were to advance from the hospital along the main road and the 1st Battalion was to move at the same time along the lower road on the embankment and swing left for the bridge.

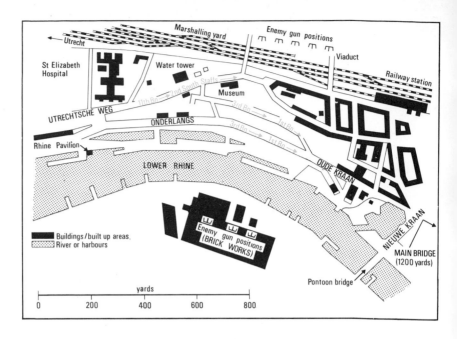

Inside Arnhem. the advance from the St Elizabeth hospital.

Fitch was now informed of his colleagues' intentions and the 3rd at about half strength took up its positions behind the 1st Battalion. Zero hour was timed for 04.00 hours and the distance to be covered was 3,000 yards.

As McCardie's South Staffords moved forward in the darkness uncanny spells of silence were broken regularly by savage bursts of firing from all four sides. The battalion front was merely the width of the street and the upstairs rooms of the houses provided galleries for the Germans to drop machine-gun fire and grenades on to the heads of the advancing troops. As the dawn broke the opposition stiffened with long-range fire descending from the high ground on the left flank but 'A' Company almost succeeded in breaking through to the centre of Arnhem. The South Staffords occupied a museum until evicted by mortars, 20-mm guns and self-propelled guns. After this short-lived success by the British troops more Panzers poured into the town to seal off the remnants of the bridge defenders. Then tanks swept down the road to the St Elizabeth Hospital decimating the South Staffords and Lea's 11th Battalion. Only a small, mixed party of men escaped to the outskirts of Arnhem; McCardie and Lea were both wounded and fell into enemy hands.

By 07.00 hours Dobie's 1st Battalion moving into a similar avenue of fire on the lower road had virtually ceased to exist. Although due to earlier losses the battalion started well below strength only forty-nine men were left standing at this time. Fitch gave the 3rd Battalion the order to retire to form a defensive line at the Rhine Pavilion but only a handful of men evaded the oncoming tanks. Dobie was wounded and taken prisoner but escaped his captors after a few days – Fitch was killed by a mortar bomb. Organised resistance at the bridge ended on Thursday, 21st September. John Frost then gave orders for over 200 wounded paratroopers of whom

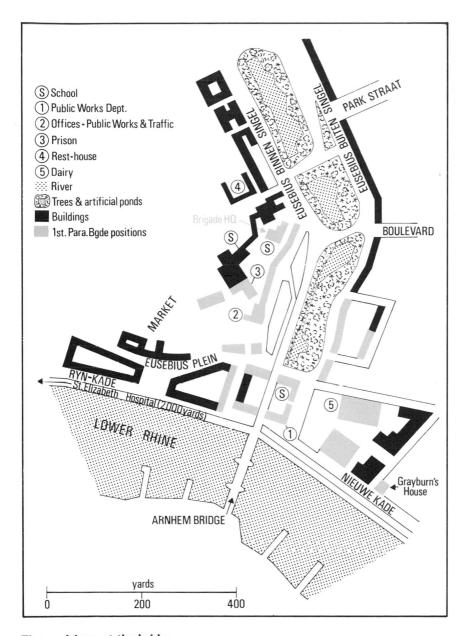

Legend:

- (S) School
- (1) Public Works Dept.
- (2) Offices - Public Works & Traffic
- (3) Prison
- (4) Rest-house
- (5) Dairy
- River
- Trees & artificial ponds
- Buildings
- 1st. Para. Bgde positions

EUSEBIUS BINNEN SINGEL

EUSEBIUS BUITEN SINGEL

PARK STRAAT

Brigade HQ

BOULEVARD

MARKET

EUSEBIUS PLEIN

RYN-KADE

St. Elizabeth Hospital (2000 yards)

LOWER RHINE

NIEUWE KADE

Grayburn's House

ARNHEM BRIDGE

yards

0   200   400

The positions at the bridge

he was one to be handed over to the Germans. About half of his force had been killed and wounded and the majority of the rest were captured making a fighting withdrawal. Those few who escaped were helped by members of the Dutch Resistance to cross the river.

Black Tuesday (the 19th) was really the day that set the seal on 1st Airborne's misfortunes. At Spanhoe and Cottesmore in England the Polish Parachute Brigade was already emplaned when adverse weather

Above.
6-pounder gun and
crew in action.

Left.
Glider pilots opening
a supply pannier.

Right.
Major-General R. E.
Urquhart, GOC 1st
Airborne Division.
He is standing in
the grounds of the
Hartenstein Hotel.

conditions forced a postponement of their drop for twenty-four hours.
The thirty-five Polish gliders were airborne that day, however, and were met
over LZ 'L' north of Johanna Hoeve by murderous anti-aircraft fire from
all types of German guns. The gliders flew in at all angles and from every
direction. Some were on fire before they landed; jeeps with punctured petrol
tanks flooded the wooden fuselages and red hot flak turned them into
flaming infernos. The Poles swarmed out of their gliders, blowing off the
tails with explosive charges in their anxiety to unload their equipment.
This Polish contingent's job was mainly to provide anti-tank support for
their own brigade but in the circumstances the troops moved south in a
fast-moving column of jeeps, trailers and 6-pounders to Oosterbeek.

Another setback occurred in the afternoon when 163 supply aircraft of Nos 38 and 46 Groups flew steadily through deadly flak to deposit their cargoes on SDP 'V' north of Warnsborn. This zone lay to the east of Johanna Hoeve and was not under the control of the airborne troops. Signals to base requesting new SDPs had not been received and the pilots dropped 390 tons of food and ammunition to the waiting Germans. The British troops north of Oosterbeek, who could see the drop, were speechless with disappointment. Leaping from their foxholes and slit trenches, they tried desperately to attract the aircrews' attention but to no avail. The drop actually took eight minutes and during this time the RAF pilots and RASC despatchers displayed incredible bravery in pursuing their fruitless tasks. Thirteen of the aircraft were shot down and ninety-seven damaged by flak shells. One Dakota aircraft piloted by Flight-Lieutenant David Lord DFC was hit by flak and the starboard wing burst into flames. As the plane lost height the pilot kept a steady onward course dropping the bulk of his supplies accurately before clearing the dropping point. Lord then turned his aircraft and flew in again to drop his remaining loads before crashing in flames. Flight-Lieutenant Lord of 271 Squadron was posthumously awarded one of the five Victoria Crosses won so deservedly for gallant conduct during the Battle of Arnhem.

Major-General Urquhart now reappeared in the main stream of fighting based on Oosterbeek. The divisional commander had actually entered Arnhem on the 18th with Brigadier Lathbury and Fitch's 3rd Battalion sweeping down the road past the St Elizabeth Hospital to the Rhine Pavilion. Here Urquhart and Lathbury with part of 1st Brigade HQ (the other part was at the bridge) had sought the refuge of a three-storeyed villa. When the 3rd Battalion advanced along the railway line in the afternoon, some of them remained pinned down in the houses adjoining the general's temporary abode. The incumbents in a state of siege – with the brigadier employed as a rifleman – hurled Gammon bombs out of the windows destroying two tanks before more armoured vehicles trundled up the road to blast them out. Urquhart and Lathbury preceded by two young officers escaped by the back door in the nick of time and ran through the cobbled streets in the direction of the St Elizabeth Hospital. Lathbury fell hit by a burst from a Spandau and was dragged into a house where he was left in the care of a brave Dutch couple. Before leaving the house Urquhart spotted a German soldier peering through the window and the general shot him dead with his automatic pistol. The three fugitives moved on to another safe house and took it in turns to keep watch from the window of their hiding place in the attic. During the night a self-propelled gun approached and the crew parked their vehicle outside the front door of the house. In the morning the vehicle drove off and the general was glad to meet a patrol of South Staffords coming up the street.

General Urquhart's headquarters had been established in his absence at the Hartenstein Hotel in Oosterbeek. When later on Black Tuesday the general arrived at the hotel, he was faced with several unpleasant decisions. The 4th Brigade, which had been savaged after the Polish glider landing, was holding its ground north of Oosterbeek but Urquhart quickly realised that a link-up with the bridge defenders was out of the question. But his assignment was to capture the Arnhem road bridge and to form a bridgehead for the Second Army across the Lower Rhine! General Urquhart now ordered his division to concentrate in a perimeter measuring four square miles based on Oosterbeek. This decision taken two days before Frost's surrender meant of course the abandonment of the paratroopers in Arnhem. The withdrawal to the Oosterbeek perimeter was intended in theory as a means of maintaining, if not a bridgehead, at least a reception zone for the Second Army on the north bank of the river. In practice for 1st Airborne, *it was a matter of survival.*

On 17th September Major-General Allan Adair's Guards Armoured Division moved off supported by a heavy artillery barrage and spent the night in Valkenswaard. On the following day the Irish Guards advancing along the road on a 'one-tank front' passed through Eindhoven and after repairing the bridge at Zon went on to cross the Veghel and Grave bridges. 101st Airborne had taken all their objectives. The tanks drove on to discover that the 82nd Airborne had taken the Maas-Waal canal bridge to the south of Nijmegen but not the road and railway bridges to the north of the town. These last two obstacles were captured after bitter fighting on the 21st by the American paratroopers and three battalions of Grenadier and Irish Guardsmen. Horrocks' XXX Corps was then less than ten miles from the Lower Rhine but the impetus of the attack quickly petered out. The road from Eindhoven, which was christened 'Hell's Highway', came under heavy flank attack during the next seven days, and Horrocks' slender supply line was cut in several places. Units of the 43rd Division pressed through the Guards and reached the south bank of the river: artillery was moved into range of the Arnhem area; but even if the road bridge had been placed at their disposal, the Second Army would have been in no position to exploit the situation.

General Urquhart chose to pitch his stumps in the Oosterbeek perimeter for three reasons. Firstly Mackenzie's Airborne Light Regiment was already sited in the neighbourhood and his 75-mm howitzers were in fact giving some support to the troops in Arnhem. Secondly Div HQ was firmly established at the Hartenstein and there was no reason to move it. Thirdly there was the question of how best to reroute Sosabowski's Polish Brigade still in England into the perimeter. The only possible dropping zones for the Poles were south of the river and Driel was finally chosen for the drop as it lay south of Oosterbeek near the Heveadorp ferry. (The ferry on the Driel side fell into German hands on the Wednesday night but the Poles after two flight cancellations due to the weather dropped as ordered on the following day.) On the 20th the perimeter looked like the thumb of the right hand jutting northwards from the river bank. The artillery site was positioned to the north of Oosterbeek and to the south of Div HQ lay No Man's Land.

The 21st Independent Parachute Company took post in the north-west corner of the perimeter. On their left and to the north of the gunner batteries came Payton-Reid's 7th KOSB. After keeping the Polish glider zone free the Scottish troops now reduced to 270 men withdrew south of the railway line to the grounds of a private hotel. This hotel, which was eventually reduced to rubble, was the centre of fierce hand-to-hand fighting during the course of the battle. The regimental records of the King's Own Scottish Borderers refer simply to the hotel as 'The White

House'. The north-eastern corner of the perimeter was occupied by the 156th and 10th Battalions of 4th Parachute Brigade. The western half was manned by three skeleton companies of the 1st Borders, the Polish glider troops and some engineers. In the south-east Urquhart gave the command of the survivors of the 1st, 3rd, South Staffords, and 11th Battalions to Major Dickie Lonsdale, the former second-in-command of the 11th Battalion. Lonsdale Force numbering about 400 men was stationed near Oosterbeek church. Finally the Glider Pilot Regiment held two positions, one at the artillery site and one in a wood further north.

After the collapse of the resistance at the bridge, Harzer assumed overall command of the German operation west of Arnhem and the Panzers unleashed their full fury on Urquhart's defences. The battle developed into a non-stop series of attacks usually launched simultaneously from two sides of the perimeter. Periods of mortaring and shelling were followed by tank attacks with infantry operating in strong patrols of from twenty to thirty men. Oosterbeek was turned into a suburban battlefield: the built-up area was rapidly devastated by high explosive and phosphorus shells; the incendiaries at first burning slowly and then more quickly until whole buildings were consumed by fire. At times fifty mortar bombs a minute fell into the area. In spite of their superior cover many of the German infantry soldiers were openly terrified at the idea of infiltrating the perimeter. The airborne troops made good use of their Vickers machine-guns, 2-in and 3-in mortars and sharpshooters took a heavy toll of German snipers perched in the trees. The British anti-tank guns were knocked out one by one but Piats fired at point blank range proved effective against the tanks.

On the withdrawal from Arnhem, the South Staffords were rallied by Major R. H. Cain, who led a successful attack on Den Brink, the wooded hill position commanding the Oosterbeek-Arnhem road. The South Staffords then took up their positions as ordered in front of the white church in

Two German prisoners brew up under guard. The prisoner on the right is dressed in a sniper's outfit.

Oosterbeek. Almost at once they saw tanks and self-propelled guns edging up to them. Lance-Sergeant J. D. Baskeyfield, who was in charge of one of the 6-pounders, destroyed two Tigers and at least one self-propelled gun from a range of 100 yards. After intense fire was sent in his direction, Baskeyfield found that he was the only member of the crew left standing; he continued to load and fire the gun himself until it was put out of action. This gallant NCO although himself wounded then crawled to another 6-pounder, the crew of which were dead, and engaged a self-propelled gun. He stopped firing temporarily to help another wounded soldier but returned to his post shortly afterwards and destroyed the SP gun. Lance-Sergeant Baskeyfield, who was killed by a tank shell, was posthumously awarded the Victoria Cross; he was twenty-one years of age.

The Germans made their first determined attempt to break into the perimeter on the 21st but were defeated at bayonet point by the 1st Borders. In the north, tanks and armoured cars prowled through the woods and enemy snipers and machine-gunners climbed up into the trees. The KOSB again resorted to their bayonets to capture 'The White House', which changed hands several times during the day. The 4th Brigade were the hardest hit: casualty returns on the 22nd showed that the 156th Battalion was down to one hundred men and the 10th having lost all its officers possessed a mere thirty men. Sir Richard de B. des Voeux. was dead and Kenneth Smyth, who was badly hurt by falling masonry, died a few days later. The RAF flew in again and succeeded in making a supply drop but suffered twenty per cent. losses in aircraft. (During the Battle of Arnhem only seven per cent. of the air supplies fell into 1st Airborne's hands.) The Polish Brigade arrived over their DZ in the afternoon and dropped to slight opposition but as no boats and rafts were available to convey them across the river, Sosabowski formed a defensive area at Driel. Here the Polish paratroopers were soon in touch with XXX Corps units: Horrocks convened a conference that was attended by Sosabowski, Browning and Thomas, commander of the 43rd Division; but although it was decided to send men across the river, all hopes of establishing a bridgehead on the north bank were abandoned.

General Urquhart at this time had no means of knowing the Second Army's revised intentions but their presence across the water boosted 1st Airborne's morale. At Oosterbeek the twice-wounded Major Dickie Lonsdale called in his force to give them the news that British tanks were on the south bank of the river. Lonsdale force wearily made their way to the shattered church. Inside the church, Lonsdale, a veteran of the Primosole action in Sicily, surveyed the upturned, unshaven faces of his expectant congregation from the pulpit. The troops had been without rations and sleep for four days and were covered from head to toe with the grime of the battlefield. His sermon, a version of which was later scrawled on the church door, was very much to the point:

'You know as well as I do that there are a lot of bloody Germans coming at us. Well, all we can do is to stay here and hang on in the hope that somebody catches us up. We must fight for our lives and stick together. We have fought them in North Africa, Sicily, Italy. At times against odds. They were not good enough for us then, and they are not bloody well good enough for us now. An hour from now you will take up defensive

Arnhem Personalities

Brigadier G. W. Lathbury, 1st Parachute Brigade.

Brigadier P. H. W. Hicks, 1st (Air-Landing) Brigade.

Brigadier R. G. Loder-Symonds, Commander Royal Artillery.

Lieutenant-Colonel D. T. Dobie, 1st Parachute Battalion.

Major R. H. Cain VC, 2nd South Staffords.

Major R. T. H. Lonsdale, Lonsdale Force.

Major B. A. Wilson, 21st Independent Parachute Company.

Major J. E. E. Linton, 2nd A/L Lt Bty RA

Captain the Rev R. Talbot Watkins, Padre 1st Parachute Battalion.

137

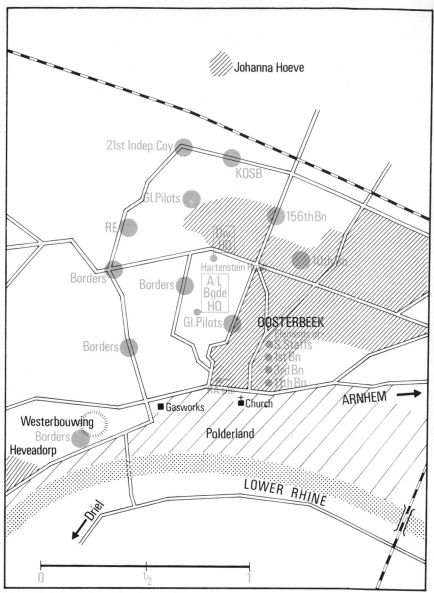

The withdrawal to the Oosterbeek perimeter on 20th September.

positions to the north of the road outside. On these positions we must stand or fall and shoot to the last round. Make certain you dig in well and that your weapons and ammo. are in good order. We are getting short of ammo., so when you shoot, you shoot to kill. Good luck to you all.'

On the 23rd the focus of the German onslaught was shifted to Lonsdale's sector. Major Robert Cain of the South Staffords, the fifth recipient of the Victoria Cross in the Battle of Arnhem, was the only one of the five to live to tell the tale. After leading the attack at Den Brink, Cain on the next day fired a Piat at twenty yards immobilising a Tiger tank from the cover of a ruined house. Although wounded by machine-gun fire and

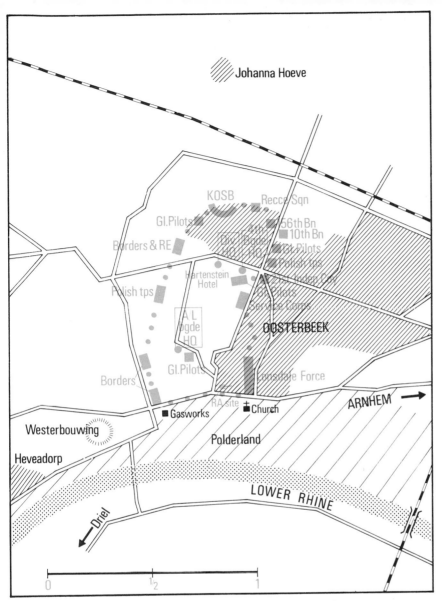

Johanna Hoeve

KOSB
Recce Sqn
Gl.Pilots
156th Bn
10th Bn
Borders & RE
Gl.Pilots
Hartenstein
Hotel
Polish tps
Polish tps
OOSTERBEEK
A L
bgde
HQ
Borders
Gl.Pilots
Lonsdale Force
RA site + Church
ARNHEM →
Gasworks
Westerbouwing
Polderland
Heveadorp

LOWER RHINE

← Driel

0   ½   1

The Oosterbeek perimeter prior to the evacuation from the north bank of the river.

collapsing brickwork, he moved out and brought up a 75-mm gun, destroying the tank completely. Now several days later as enemy pressure increased, Cain drove off three tanks with a Piat and on the 25th he manned a 2-in mortar and repelled an attack mounted by SPs and infantry carrying flame-throwers. Major Cain, who early on in the proceedings was deafened by a perforated eardrum, received the award for his inspired leadership and great personal bravery selflessly displayed throughout the battle.

The airborne troops now received some fire support from external sources. Spitfires and Typhoons escorting the persistent supply aircraft peeled off from their formations to strafe the German gun positions. South of the river on the 23rd a signaller belonging to a gunner regiment picked up a voice message from Oosterbeek on his wireless set: 'We are being heavily shelled and mortared. Can you help us?' A 4.5-in battery immediately reported 'ready' and airborne OPs started directing a steady stream of shells at enemy targets. The gunners quickly erected a 25-ft wireless aerial for better reception and then added to the volume of fire with two batteries of 5.5-in and 155-mm guns.

The edges of the Oosterbeek perimeter were being steadily eroded and the Panzers by the end of the week had taken a large chunk out of the north-eastern sector. On the 24th the 4th Brigade, or what was left of it, had fallen back on the 1st Borders' area and 1st Airborne's lines in fact encompassed a zone of about one square mile extending to the west and north-west of the village. The St Elizabeth Hospital in Arnhem continued to receive British, German and civilian casualties throughout the battle; the Dutch and captive airborne doctors working under the watchful eyes of the SS guards. (The SS, however, had no stomach for surgery and they soon departed their posts in the operating theatres.) The Dutch nurses worked with such efficiency and devotion to duty that clean sheets were put on the beds every day. Inside the perimeter, the 181st (Air-Landing) and 133rd (Parachute) Field Ambulances, which had originally been set up independently at Wolfhezen, were combined as one unit in Oosterbeek. The airborne medical services helped by local doctors were established in nine hotels, public buildings and private houses. Casualties were mounting daily and it was estimated at one stage that over one thousand men were lying in the hospital area awaiting treatment.

Such food as was received from Air Supply was given to the wounded. After the first day there were no more rations for the fit men; some made soup from vegetables collected from the fields and others ate raw potatoes. The forbearance, kindness and courage of the people of Oosterbeek were great sources of help and inspiration to the airborne troops. Many civilians

Below
British prisoners are hustled away.

Below right
A Dutch nurse attends to wounded troops in Oosterbeek.

willingly exposed themselves to great risks conveying military messages and reporting on German movement. In one private house used as a medical post, a Dutch lady, Mrs Ter Horst, who was to see her home destroyed, nursed the wounded and went amongst them, her bible in her hand, reading from the Psalms. The field ambulances on the 24th were completely overrun: an operating theatre installed at the Hotel de Tafelberg collapsed under bombardment; and the second surgical unit at the Hotel Schoonhord was captured by German infantry. The airborne chaplains gave magnificent service in comforting the wounded; of the original party of fifteen chaplains, two of them, the Rev H. J. Irwin and Father Benson, were killed in action; three were taken prisoner and when the fighting was over seven of them elected to accompany the wounded into captivity.

At the Hartenstein Hotel, which had taken its share of the battering, Urquhart and his staff were working in the cellars by candlelight. On the 22nd (Friday), the general sent Lieutenant-Colonel C. B. Mackenzie, his GSO I, and Lieutenant-Colonel E. C. W. Myers, his chief engineer officer, across the Lower Rhine to report the worsening situation to General Horrocks. After crossing the river in an inflatable dinghy these officers returned on the following night and communicated the Second Army's decision to remain on the south bank. General Dempsey and his commanders were of the opinion, however, that the airborne perimeter should be reinforced before attempting a withdrawal. A small party from the 3rd Polish Parachute Battalion had already succeeded in crossing the river in small boats and on rafts and on the night of the 23rd 5th Bn the Dorset Regiment and more Polish paratroopers made another attempt to cross over by similar means.

The Dorsets did not start before midnight, by which time it was pretty obvious to the Germans where the assault would take place. The Germans had been sending mortar and artillery fire across the river into the Polish

Survivors on the south side of the river.

Brigade's position at Driel, and it came as no surprise to the former when they saw boats crossing near the Heveadorp Ferry. Murderous machine-gun fire raked the boats and wounded men were carried screaming down the swiftly flowing river. Some Dorsets and a few Poles reached the north bank but well to the west of Oosterbeek. The commanding officer of the 1st Borders, Lieutenant-Colonel Hadden, was one of the men who safely crossed the river. His glider had crash-landed in England on the first day of 'Market-Garden' and he suffered a similar fate near Antwerp on the second glider lift. After finding his way to Nijmegen, he eagerly joined the river assault party in an effort to rejoin his battalion. He did but was taken prisoner.

When General Urquhart read a letter conveyed by Myers from Major-General G. I. Thomas of the 43rd Division explaining the Second Army's decision, he immediately drew up his plans to pull out of the perimeter. On Myers and his sappers fell the task of finding and improvising river craft and selecting the embarkation points; Thomas also promised to help by sending sappers with light boats across the river. The fighting continued unabated on the 24th and well into the 25th when at 18.30 hours the officers were told to prepare to move. Urquhart's plan was to evacuate his northern positions first gradually progressing southwards so that the men nearest the river bank would be the last to leave. Some of the wounded were to be taken with them but there was no alternative but to leave the majority of them behind. The doctors volunteered to a man to stay. The escapers blackened their faces and muffled their boots and loose equipment was tied tightly to the body. The glider pilots were posted as guides along the western and eastern extremities of the escape corridor. The withdrawal was due to commence at 22.00 hours. The distance to be covered from the northern outposts to the river was approximately two miles.

It was raining fairly heavily when the first men left their posts. No one spoke and luckily the rain helped to mask the sounds of movement. The men moved cautiously in single files each man holding on to the smock of the man in front. A cryptic message passed in the afternoon to Urquhart's headquarters contained the details of 43rd Division's fire plan to cover the evacuation and the British gunners now opened up as scheduled on the enemy positions flanking the perimeter. Fortunately for 1st Airborne the Germans did not know they were going but even so desultory shell and mortar fire straddled their lines of retreat. The men were halted in their tracks by the occasional sounds of small arms and machine-gun fire. The sappers had performed wonders in assembling the river craft but inevitably there were not enough to go round. When the last boat had gone about 500 men were left behind; some plunged into the river and others went off in a hopeless search for other crossing points. As just one example of individual courage displayed during the evacuation, the Rev R. Talbot Watkins, a Methodist minister from Leeds and one of three padres to escape, led a party of fifty wounded men safely across to the south bank; he then returned to help more of the wounded but found no one. After spending the day hiding from German patrols, he swam across the river and rejoined the airborne survivors at Nijmegen.

Operation 'Market-Garden' had not turned the flank of Hitler's West Wall: the big pursuit from the Seine was over and four months went by before the Canadian First Army attacked at Nijmegen and advanced up the west bank of the Rhine. General Urquhart brought less than 3,000 of the original 10,005 men landed on the 17th and 18th out of the Battle of Arnhem. During the battle 5,000 men including 3,000 wounded went into captivity. 550 men were listed as killed in action but the number of dead was far greater as 1,500 of the men posted as missing did not return. (The cemetery at Oosterbeek, which over the years has been cared for with great devotion by the local people, contains 1,500 white crosses.) The Polish Brigade north and south of the river suffered 500 casualties. Of Urquhart's brigadiers, Lathbury and Hackett were held prisoner in the St Elizabeth Hospital but Hicks crossed the river: the toll of battalion commanders was severe, Fitch, des Voeux and Smyth were dead; McCardie, Lea, Frost and Hadden were prisoners; only Payton-Reid and later Dobie reached Nijmegen. About two hundred men were at large on the north bank for several weeks before falling prisoner or crossing the river with the help of the Dutch Resistance.

Soon after the battle was over 1st Airborne moved back from Nijmegen to Louvain and thence across the Channel to the United Kingdom. Much has been written about Arnhem since the war; *a posteriori* judgements may enhance the historian's style but seldom his reputation. General Urquhart's plan was a thesis of no alternatives. The aircraft problem prevented concentration in strength on the first day. Further, the adverse weather conditions after the 17th caused delays in the arrival of the 4th and Polish Brigades and hindered supply arrangements. The opposition was obviously underestimated but one wonders what difference it would have made to the airborne commitment if the enemy dispositions had in fact been accurately assessed. 'Market Garden' did not come off but for reasons other than the airborne failure to capture the Arnhem area. The red devils went to Arnhem expecting to be relieved in two days but held on north of the river for nine days and nine nights. This against such determined opposition was a superhuman effort.

On the German side, the speed of reaction of Bittrich's Panzer Corps in the declining circumstances of the German Army was a credit to their military organization. The post-war myth that the airborne plan was betrayed has been finally refuted. Harzer's Hohenstaufen Division fought a ruthless battle but behaved with chivalry towards their prisoners. The German opinion of the British airborne troops was summed up in these few words from Sepp Krafft's battle report. 'They were well trained, particularly for independent fighting and of good combat value.' The officers graded up in rank according to age were the finest in the whole British Army. Very well schooled, personally hard, persevering and brave, they made an outstanding impression.' Sources of motivation, however, puzzled the Germans. They themselves still took their politics seriously but apparently the British were not similarly controlled. In this matter the graffiti scrawled on the gliders only led to a deepening sense of bewilderment. Here are three of the inscriptions Krafft quoted for posterity:

WE ARE THE AL CAPONE GANG
UP THE REDS
UP WITH THE FRÄULEINS' SKIRTS

Street fighting in Athens.

Operation 'Manna'

On 12th October 1944, 2nd Independent Parachute Brigade launched Operation 'Manna', an airborne landing in Greece. Flying from Brindisi in southern Italy, Coxen's 4th Parachute Battalion Group was quickly followed into Megara by the 5th and 6th Battalions. Megara airfield, one of Student's emplaning points for the invasion of Crete, lies a short distance from Athens and Brigadier Pritchard led his men into the Greek capital a few days later. Although the Germans were rapidly retreating northwards peace had not come to Athens. Communal riots and fighting between political parties were rife, but Arkforce (2nd Brigade and 23rd Armoured Brigade) was not at first involved in the incidents. In October parachute units were pursuing the Germans in Thrace, Salonika and on the Bulgarian frontier but soon involvement in the insurrection in Athens was unavoidable. The ELAS faction in Athens was officially outlawed on 7th December and driven out of the city by Arkforce after four weeks of vicious street fighting. 2nd Independent Parachute Brigade returned to Italy at the end of January 1945; thirty airborne operations were planned to support the Eighth Army in northern Italy, but all were cancelled. The brigade sailed for England on 16th June and its battalions stood down after three years' service on 31st August 1945.

The Ardennes and the Rhine-crossing

After Operation 'Market-Garden' Lieutenant-General Browning was posted to Ceylon to take up his appointment as Chief of Staff to Lord Louis Mountbatten, Supreme Allied Commander, South East Asia Command. Major-General R. N. Gale now took Browning's place as Deputy Commander First Allied Airborne Army. The post of Colonel Commandant the Parachute Regiment, which had been held since 1942 by Field-Marshal Dill, was taken up at this time by Field-Marshal Montgomery. Gale was succeeded as GOC 6th Airborne Division by Major-General E. L. Bols, whose substantive rank was that of Colonel. 6th Airborne arrived in North West Europe again on Boxing Day 1944 and hastened across snow-covered Belgium to cover the Meuse crossings between Namur and Dinant. Hitler's last bow in the Ardennes offensive had been universally applauded but now the curtain had fallen and when the 3rd, 5th and Air-Landing Brigades advanced against the tip of the salient the Germans were already pulling out. In the last week in January the division was transferred to Holland and took up positions on the River Maas [Meuse] between Roermond and Venlo. On 24th February 6th Airborne Division was back again in England but not for long. Operation 'Varsity' on 24th March was destined to take them beyond the Rhine into Germany.

The plan for Operation 'Varsity' was based on a new concept for the employment of airborne troops. Brereton's First Allied Airborne Army was to land not before but after land operations had begun. Montgomery's 21st Army Group striking from south of the Waal was to send Commandos spearheading infantry and armoured elements across the Rhine to capture Wesel. The airborne rôle after the initial bombardment was to seize high ground crowned by a wood, the Diersfordter Wald, and deny the enemy observation posts overlooking the bridgehead; further objectives included the capture of bridges to the north of Wesel to prevent enemy movement towards the river. The crossing was to be made by the British Second Army with the United States Ninth Army on the right. General Matthew B. Ridgway's US 18th Airborne Corps consisting of the British 6th and US 17th Airborne Divisions (Bols and Miley) was nominated as the airborne task force. Gale was appointed as Ridgway's deputy.

Dempsey's Second Army started crossing the Rhine between Xanten

A jeep and 20-mm Oerlikon gun move off after landing in a Horsa glider.

Major-General Eric Bols, the new GOC 6th Airborne Division.

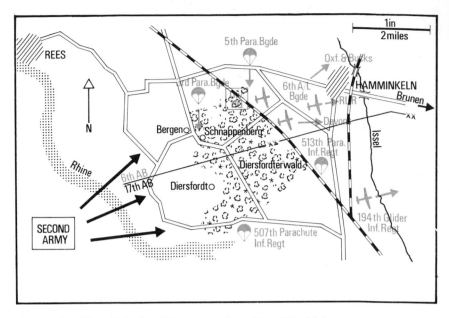

Operation 'Varsity': the Rhine-crossing. The 18th Airborne Corps plan.

and Rees soon after nightfall on 23rd March. Shortly after daybreak on the 24th, 1,696 transport planes and 1,348 gliders brought 21,680 Allied airborne troops to the battlefield in one single lift. The skytrain run by the US 9th Troop Carrier Command and Nos 38 and 46 Groups RAF was escorted by nearly one thousand fighter aircraft and twice that number supported the ground operations. The fly-in lasted two hours and forty minutes and at times the anti-aircraft fire was devastating. The aircraft types this time included the C-46 Commando, which enabled the troops to jump from port and starboard doors. The C-46s when hit were liable to burst into flames and twenty-two of them were lost in this manner. (If a wing tank was punctured the fuel ran down the fuselage, and an incendiary shell would set the whole aircraft aflame in a second.) Altogether forty-four transport planes and eighty gliders were destroyed by the anti-aircraft gunners.

The British Division was to secure the northern half of the Corps zone. Bols' specific objectives were the capture of the high ground covered by the Diersfordter Wald east of Bergen, the town of Hamminkeln and some of the bridges over the River Issel. Hill's 3rd Parachute Brigade dropped north of Schnappenberg on the western edge of the area. The 8th Battalion, which was first on the ground, suffered losses on the DZ from light anti-aircraft weapons used as field guns. The anger of the 1st Canadian Parachute Battalion was aroused when the men found their commanding officer, Lieutenant-Colonel J. S. Nicklin, hanging dead from a tree. Nicklin had been shot by a German marksman while attempting to free himself from his parachute harness. The 8th Battalion remained engaged on the DZ while the 1st Canadian and 9th Battalions seized Schnappenberg. In the mid-afternoon the 3rd Brigade linked with ground forces advancing from the river. A Canadian medical orderly, Corporal Frederick Topham, was awarded the Victoria Cross for gallant conduct during the landings.

Poett's 5th Parachute Brigade dropped from about 1,000 feet and had consequently to contend with air bursts and small arms fire on the way down. The 7th, 12th and 13th Battalions landed astride a road ˙eading into Hamminkeln and by late afternoon had captured their objectives. 6th (Air-Landing) Brigade now commanded by Brigadier R. H. Bellamy landed east of the Diersfordter Wald. The gliders came in through a haze of smoke and dust raised by the Second Army's bombardment; the 2nd Oxf. and Bucks captured the key bridges over the Issel; the 12th Devons and 1st RUR moving into Hamminkeln. The village was taken with the help of the American 513th Parachute Infantry Regiment.

Operation 'Varsity' was not entirely necessary. Late on the 24th, the Second Army was streaming unopposed across the Rhine. The Allied airborne troops had accomplished their tasks but their success did not justify the losses. The heavy toll of carrier aircraft and gliders has already been quoted. Forty-one aircrew were killed, 153 wounded and 163 posted as missing. 6th Airborne Division lost 347 men killed and 731 wounded and the 17th Airborne lost 159 killed and 522 wounded. About 1,000 British and American troops were reported missing but many of them found their way back to their lines.

The advance from the Rhine to the Baltic.

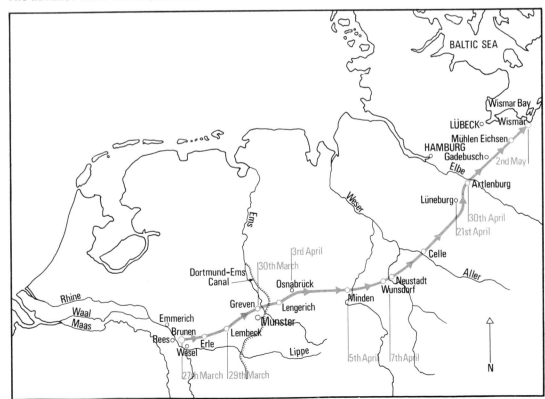

Warm greetings on a
cold morning in
Germany. Brigadier
James Hill, 3rd
Parachute Brigade,
receives the Silver
Star from General
'Matt' Ridgway,
Commander 18th
Airborne Corps.
Field-Marshal
Montgomery looks
on.

The Race to the Baltic

As the Second Army passed through, 6th Airborne was ordered to advance in the van of Montgomery's drive into Germany. The division was deservedly chosen to lead but how the troops were to keep pace with such a modest allocation of transport was a matter for urgent consideration.

When the advance began with air support on 26th March, the red devils seized all the vehicles they could lay their hands on. Four wheels and an engine were preferred but a war correspondent reported sighting an airborne soldier mounted on a steamroller. A BBC news broadcast even informed its listeners that parachute troops had been seen moving forward pushing perambulators piled high with equipment. 4th Tank Battalion, Grenadier Guards, was sent to their aid and one medium and two field regiments of artillery were assigned for fire support. Between 26th March and 2nd May, 6th Airborne fighting as infantry of the line travelled 350 miles from Hamminkeln to the Baltic coast. The forward route took them across the River Ems, and the Weser, through Lüneburg and over the Elbe to Wismar. 5th Parachute Brigade started off but the 3rd passed through them on 28th March to capture Lembeck. Two days later 1st Canadian Parachute Battalion seized the Ems crossing at Greven after a night attack.

The 5th Brigade occupied Osnabrück and the 3rd on 7th April covered seventy miles from Greven to Minden in thirty-six hours. After clearing Wunsdorf progress across the Aller to the Elbe was not so swift. On 30th April the Allied bridgeheads on the Elbe between Tesperhude and Bleckede were twelve miles wide. This sector was held on the left by the British VIII Corps including 11th Armoured Division and on the right by Ridgway's Airborne Corps. General Dempsey made known his wish that the British airborne division should be given priority in the break-out. Ridgway for sound tactical reasons refused but later relented when he realised the reason for the request. The airborne's pride had been badly shattered at Arnhem and Dempsey wanted the prestige of the link-up with the Russians to go to the red devils. Although Ridgway agreed to turn them loose there was no time to change the plan of advance. The Elbe bridges at Artlenburg and Lauenburg were initially reserved for 11th Armoured Division and 6th Airborne now with tanks of the Royal Scots Greys under command were placed low on the list.

The British paratroopers soon solved their own problem. They turned their red berets inside out so that the black linings made them look like armoured troops and draped the Shermans with camouflage netting to hide the tactical signs. The military police at the bridges eyed the troops riding on the tanks suspiciously but accepted that they belonged to units of 11th Armoured Division. 3rd Parachute Brigade led in this manner but both the 3rd and the 5th were across the Elbe on 1st May. The first elements of 6th Airborne – eleven tanks bearing men of 1st Canadian Parachute Battalion – arrived in Wismar, a seaport town, at 13.00 hours on the following day. The 3rd Brigade spread out through the town but the inhabitants had barricaded themselves in fearing that the Russians would arrive first. The British troops suspected a trap but after a thorough search they realised that the town was undefended. Before nightfall, a party of Russian soldiers drove cautiously into Wismar. The occupants of the vehicles relaxed when they saw the British uniforms and after gestures of goodwill from both sides, the Russians drove off the way they had come. The red devils had won the race to the Baltic by eight hours.

For 6th Airborne Division the war in Europe was over. VE Day was spent on the Baltic coast, a long way from their home on the Salisbury Plain. Since D-Day, 6th June 1944, casualties had totalled 1,520 dead, 3,459 wounded and 1,302 missing.

1st Airborne Division after its heavy losses at Arnhem was reorganised and was ready to take part in the liberation of Denmark and Norway. On 10th May 1st Airborne less 1st Parachute Brigade but reinforced by the Special Air Service Brigade flew from England to Norway to engage in security duties. The 1st Brigade was already in Denmark *en route* for Norway. On 21st May General Urquhart's headquarters was re-designated HQ Norway Command. Some 6,000 airborne troops were landed in Norway where the German garrison numbered about 350,000 men. General Urquhart was responsible for receiving their surrender and was at first in charge of Norwegian civil affairs. 1st Airborne Division was withdrawn from Norway on 24th August 1945 and was officially disbanded just over two months later.

Appendix 1 The Special Air Service Regiment

David Stirling, the founder of the Special Air Service Regiment. The regimental motto is 'Who Dares Wins'.

'L' Detachment, Special Air Service Brigade, was raised in Egypt in July 1941. There was no brigade incidentally, only 'L' Detachment, consisting of seven officers and about sixty men. The Special Air Service (SAS) was founded by Lieutenant A. D. Stirling, Scots Guards, an officer then serving with No 3 Commando. David Stirling's military rationale differed from the official Commando line in that he believed that the *coup de main* method of striking in strength at one target in the rear of the enemy lines was wasteful of manpower and resources. Far better, suggested the young Scot, to pounce simultaneously on several targets with small bands of resourceful men. In 1941, the chain of Axis ports, staging garrisons, airfields and supply centres stretching from Tripoli to the Egyptian frontier provided many suitable objectives for SAS raiding parties.

The ranks of the SAS were strengthened by more hand-picked volunteers from other units, and in the absence in the early days of much help from Ringway, evolved their own system of parachute training. The first training jumps were made from Vickers Valentia and Bombay aircraft at Kabrit near the Great Bitter Lake. The first and last SAS parachute sortie into the desert was launched on the night of 16th November 1941, twenty-four hours in advance of General Auchinleck's offensive across the Egyptian frontier into Cyrenaica. The SAS objective was to break into five different airfields in the Gazala-Timini area and destroy fighter aircraft on the ground. Fifty-five parachutists led by David Stirling took off from Fuka airstrip in five Bombay aircraft, but atrocious winds turned the drop into a nightmare. The raid was a complete failure and only twenty-two men survived for the pick-up in vehicles by the Long Range Desert Group.

During the next eighteen months of fighting in North Africa, the SAS operated behind the Axis lines with conspicuous success but travelling in vehicles or on foot; the LRDG playing an important rôle in lifting them in trucks to and from operational areas. The SAS developed their own style of armed jeep, the main features of which were a Browning machine-gun mounted on the bonnet and pairs of either Vickers K or Lewis aircraft guns mounted in the rear of the jeep. In January 1943, 1st SAS was formed with an establishment of five squadrons and about 400 officers and men. Lieutenant-Colonel Stirling's command was equivalent in strength to a half-battalion, but his numbers were augmented by Allied volunteers of the French SAS Squadron, the Greek Sacred Squadron and the Special Boat Section. David Stirling was captured in the Sfax-Gabes area in early 1943 and taken as a prisoner to Italy; he escaped four times before the Germans locked him up as an alien VIP in Colditz for the rest of the war. 1st SAS was subsequently commanded by Lieutenant-Colonel R. B. (Paddy) Mayne, who was personally credited after the desert war with having destroyed more enemy aircraft than any of the fighter pilots.

Before the conclusion of the North African campaign 2nd SAS was formed as a unit of the British First Army and along with 1st SAS (temporarily renamed the Special Raiding Squadron) later undertook missions in Sardinia, Crete, the Greek Islands, the Dodecanese, Sicily and Italy. Stirling's brother Lieutenant-Colonel W. S. 'Bill' Stirling was the commanding officer of 2nd SAS until succeeded by Lieutenant-Colonel Brian Franks prior to SAS participation in the invasion of North West Europe. The Special Boat Section bifurcated from the main body of the SAS under the title of the Special Boat Service. The SBS, led by Lieutenant-Colonel the Earl Jellicoe, operated in the Mediterranean theatre until the end of the war.

The Special Air Service became associated with Browning's 1st Airborne

Corps in January 1944 when the Regiment, less SBS, was formed up in Ayrshire in Scotland as the Special Air Service Brigade. This time a brigade really existed: 1st SAS (Mayne) at Darvel; 2nd SAS (Stirling/Franks) near Prestwick; and close by at Galston, 3rd SAS (Conan), 4th SAS (Bourgoin) and 5th SAS (Blondeel). The 3rd and 4th were French parachute battalions and the 5th a Belgian parachute company. 'F' Squadron Phantom Signals (GHQ Reconnaissance Regiment) was attached to the brigade in March 1944 and parachute-trained at Ringway for the coming SAS undercover rôle in France, Belgium, Holland and Germany. The Phantom signallers were assigned individually to SAS parties in the field and were equipped with crystal-controlled Jed sets for long-range wireless telegraphy. The SAS Brigade was commanded by Brigadier R. W. Macleod until March 1945 when he was succeeded by Brigadier R. M. ('Mad Mike') Calvert of Chindit fame. The overall strength of the SAS at the time of the Normandy invasion was about 2,500 officers and men.

The winged dagger, the SAS cap badge. Some say the dagger was meant to be a sword.

From 6th June 1944, the SAS Brigade carried out forty-two operations behind the lines in North West Europe. The general pattern of an SAS operation, which might be phased over several months, was firstly for a base to be established in conjunction with resistance forces. Attacks were then made on enemy personnel, communications, vehicles and supply centres. The armed jeep was used with devastating effect on German convoys. Wireless contact was maintained with the UK base at 1st Airborne Corps HQ to call for reinforcements, supply drops and RAF bomber strikes. Most of the SAS expeditions were launched from 'the cage' at Fairford under the auspices of Nos 38 and 46 Group RAF. The Short Stirling was the aircraft most commonly used for the supply drops. The operational zones were at first confined to Brittany and Normandy, but as the Allies began to break out from the Normandy bridgehead, the SAS went deep into central and eastern France, Belgium and Luxembourg. After October the focus of attention switched to Holland and then to a more conventional assault rôle after the Rhine-crossing. Late in 1944, Major Roy Farran's 3rd Squadron, 2nd SAS, was sent to fight with the partisans in Northern Italy. The SAS Brigade accompanied 1st Airborne Division to Norway in May 1945.

2nd SAS near Castino in Italy.

151

Appendix 2 The Chindits

Major-General
Orde Wingate after
landing at
Broadway.

Allied airborne manoeuvre was essentially tactical in concept throughout the war. The German invasion of Crete in 1941 was of course a truly strategic operation. Paradoxically the only Allied strategic assault from the air was mounted without the assistance of recognized airborne units. It was in Burma that Major-General Orde Wingate developed an operational theory that depended entirely on air supply. In 1943 the British launched two offensives against the Japanese on the Burma front. The first, in the Arakan, was a failure. The second was a long-range penetration raid by the then Brigadier Wingate's 77th Infantry Brigade through the north of Burma. The brigade was divided into seven columns of about 400 men, and 100 mules each. These fighting columns comprising British, Gurkha and Burmese troops were known as the 'Chindits' after a legendary lion called 'Chinthé' (the 'Protector of the Pagodas'). No troops were flown into action but air supply played an important rôle in the operation. The raid, which lasted four months, achieved little success but proved that the Briton could fight as hard as the Asiatic in jungle conditions.

The Fourteenth Army did not contemplate another offensive into Burma until autumn 1944. Wingate considered that the attack would be materially assisted by airborne brigades landing in isolated groups behind the Japanese lines. Each brigade would then form a jungle stronghold as a firm base for sorties across the enemy's lines of communication. Each stronghold would be supplied from the air on a scale equal to resisting Japanese forces diverted from the main front. Wingate's ambitious plan was accepted but with the object of assisting General Stilwell's Chinese-American forces in their drive to capture Mogaung and Myitkyina. Stilwell's aim was to secure a corridor large enough to build a road and pipeline from North East Assam to Yunnan in China.

Wingate's objective was to draw off the Japanese forces on the Salween River by forming his strongholds south of Mogaung in the area of Indaw. His '3rd Indian Division' (Special Force) consisted of six brigades plus support and service troops. The Second Chindit Operation was due to commence in February 1944 and if successful would also provide the Fourteenth Army with intermediate bases for their advance as soon as the monsoon was over. A vital element of Special Force was the American Air Commando, consisting of bombers, fighters, transports and gliders, as well as light aircraft for evacuating casualties. No. 1 Air Commando was under the joint command of Colonels Philip Cochran and John Alison, USAAF.

On 5th February, the 16th British Brigade (Fergusson) began a strenuous approach march from Ledo in the Brahmaputra Valley to Indaw, a distance of 360 miles across the Upper Chindwin River and over the Patkai ranges. When Fergusson's brigade reached the Chindwin, four gliders flew in with equipment to assist the crossing. At the same time, two gliderborne patrols were landed on the far bank to secure a bridgehead. On 5th March, just as the crossing was concluded, the first wave of Brigadier Calvert's 77th Indian Brigade took off in Wacos from airfields in Assam and headed for the Irrawaddy River. Calvert's original plan had been to land north-east of Indaw and west of the river in two jungle clearings, 'Piccadilly' and 'Broadway'. Before take-off, however, an air photograph had revealed that 'Piccadilly' had been blocked by the Japanese with tree trunks. Calvert agreed to take the whole of his brigade into 'Broadway' and fifty-four gliders were airborne by early evening. The Pathfinders followed by Advance HQ landed at approximately 20.35 hours and succeeded in laying a flarepath shortly before the arrival of the main body of the first lift. These gliders were actually conveyed on 'double-tow', *ie* two per tug. Thirty-seven came down on the flarepath. Of the remaining seventeen, eleven crash-landed behind the British lines in Assam and six fell into Japanese-occupied territory. About 350 men clambered out of the gliders at 'Broadway' and were ready to fight.

Further landings were impossible until the gliders had been cleared from the runway. This was achieved by first light with the help of a bulldozer and twelve light planes flew in at noon on the first day. From then on for the next few days over one hundred Dakotas landed each night. General Wingate landed at 'Broadway' on the second night but so far no contact had been made with the enemy. Brigadier Lentaigne's 111th Indian Brigade started to arrive on the same night at 'Chowringhee': this clearing was situated south-east of Indaw and east of the Irrawaddy; but after four columns came to ground, Wingate closed the airstrip down and concentrated his reception centre at 'Broadway'. Lentaigne's force crossed the Irrawaddy on the 10th and like Fergusson's force on the Chindwin was helped by equipment brought in by gliders. Six hundred and fifty Dakota and glider sorties were flown during the first seven nights of the operation. During that time 9,000 men, 1,350 mules, field and anti-aircraft guns were safely deposited 150 miles behind the Japanese lines.

The next airborne phase involved the fly-in on 22nd March of Brodie's 14th British Brigade and Gilmore's 3rd West African Brigade. A new landing zone, code-named 'Aberdeen', was chosen north-west of Indaw in the Meza valley. By this time Fergusson's 16th Brigade had reached the same area. The 23rd British Brigade originally allocated to Special Force was now re-assigned to a short penetration raid across the Chindwin some ninety miles south-west of Indaw. By the beginning of April, Calvert's Brigade had established a stronghold astride the road and rail communications between Indaw and Mogaung. This fortified position became known as the 'White City' because of the white supply parachutes that draped the trees. In May, another stronghold ('Blackpool'), which was manned by the 111th Brigade, was set up in the Mogaung Valley.

General Wingate was killed in a plane crash on the night of 24th March and his death came as a tremendous blow to the Chindits. Under General Lentaigne, they saw much bitter fighting but were more than equal to their adversaries. The 16th Brigade was withdrawn from Burma in May but the others were in constant action until the end of June. The operations leading to the link-up with Stilwell's Chinese-American forces in late June involved the 14th, 77th and 3rd West African Brigades. Mogaung fell to the 77th Brigade on 27th June. Both the 77th and 111th, which had taken a heavy battering at 'Blackpool', were pulled out of the fighting shortly afterwards. Myitkyina did not fall to Stilwell until 3rd August. Both of the remaining Chindit brigades were flown out between 17th and 26th August.

Although the Japanese themselves had partly fulfilled Special Force's commitment of relieving pressure on Stilwell's Army by launching their last, great offensive towards the Indian frontier, the Chindits had pinned down three enemy divisions vitally needed in the front line. Lines of communication had been disrupted and Japanese morale severely undermined. When the last Chindit Brigade was pulled out in August the tide had turned on the Burma front and the Japanese Army was in full retreat across the Chindwin River.

Appendix 3 Order of Battle

1st Airborne Division

November 1941
Divisional Headquarters formed in United Kingdom w.e.f. 1st November. The Divisional Commander took over command on 4th November.

21st May – 24th August 1945
Divisional Headquarters was designated HQ Norway Command.

GOC
4th Nov. 1941 Maj.-Gen. F. A. M. Browning
6th May 1943 Maj.-Gen. G. F. Hopkinson (died of wounds 9.43)
11th Sept. 1943 Maj.-Gen. E. E. Down
10th Dec. 1943 Maj.-Gen. R. E. Urquhart

Divisional Troops
The following units served at various times during the period 11.41–11.45:

RAC
Airborne Lt Tk Sqn, 1 A/L Recce. Sqn

RE
9 Fd Coy, 261 Fd Pk Coy
1, 2, 3, 4 Para. Sqns
1, 9, 591 Airborne Sqns
261 Airborne Pk Sqn

INF.
1 A/L Recce. Sqn

SIGS
1 Airborne Div. Sigs

RA
1 A/L Lt Bty, 1 A/L Lt Regt
Atk Btys:
 204 Indep., 1 A/L, 2 A/L, 5 A/L
Atk Regt:
 1 A/L
LAA Btys:
 283, 1 A/L

AAC
21 Indep. Para. Coy (Pathfinders)

1st Parachute Brigade

September 1941. Brigade Headquarters formed in United Kingdom w.e.f. 5th September.

Commander
5th Sept. 1941 Brig. R. N. Gale
18th April 1942 Brig. E. W. C. Flavell
28th April 1943 Brig. G. W. Lathbury
19th Sept. 1944 Lt-Col. J. D. Frost (*temp.*)
23rd Oct. 1944 Brig. G. W. Lathbury
1st Jan. 1945 Brig. E. E. G. L. Searight
30th July 1945 Brig. S. J. L. Hill

Units

		Under command
1 Para. Bn	9.41–5.45	
	7.45–8.45	9.42–5.43
2 Para. Bn	9.41–5.45	1 Para. Sqn RE
	7.45–8.45	16 Para. Fd Amb.
3 Para. Bn	10.41–5.42	'J' Sec. 2 Coy Airborne Div. Signals
4 Para. Bn	1.42–7.42	
'B' Coy 13 Para. Bn	5.45	5.45–7.45
17 Para. Bn	8.45	Royals (RAC), 2 KRRC (Inf.)

nb After Arnhem the survivors of 1, 2, and 3 Para. Bns were joined up with those of 4 Para. Bgde until 11.44.

4th Parachute Brigade

December 1942. Brigade Headquarters formed in the Middle East w.e.f. 1st December.

Commander

6th Dec. 1942 Lt-Col K. B. I. Smyth (temp.)
4th Jan. 1943 Brig. J. W. Hackett
5th March 1943 Lt-Col K. B. I. Smyth (temp.)
8th April 1943 Brig. J. W. Hackett

16th Oct. 1943 Lt-Col K. B. I. Smyth (temp.)
7th Nov. 1943 Brig. J. W. Hackett
24th Sept. 1944 Lt-Col I. A. Murray (temp.)

Units

10 Para. Bn   2.43–9.44
156 Para. Bn 2.43–9.44
11 Para. Bn   4.43–5.43
              1.44–9.44

Under command
3.43–5.43
4 Para. Sqn RE
3.43–6.43
133 Fd Amb.

1st (Air-Landing) Brigade

December 1941. Brigade Headquarters formed in the United Kingdom as HQ 1st A/L Bgde Group w.e.f. 10th December 1941. Redesignated HQ 1st A/L Bgde w.e.f. 10th March 1943.

Commander

10th Dec. 1941 Brig. G. F. Hopkinson
6th April 1943 Brig. P. H. W. Hicks
11th Dec. 1944 Lt-Col R. Payton-Reid (temp.)
14th Dec. 1944 Brig. R. H. Bower

Units

1 Border   12.41–8.45
2 S Staffords 12.41–8.45
2 Oxf. Bucks. 12.41–5.43

1 RUR   12.41–5.43
7 KOSB   12.43–8.45

Under command
at various times 12.41–12.42:
RA   458 Lt Bty
      1 A/L Lt Bty
      223 Atk Bty
      1 A/L Atk Bty

RE   9 Fd Coy
INF. 1 A/L Recce. Coy
      1 A/L Recce. Sqn
ST.   1 A/L Bgde Gp Coy RASC
MED. 181 Fd Amb.
PRO. 1 A/L Bgde Gp Pro. Sec.

Locations

1 Para. Bgde		*4 Para. Bgde*		*1 A/L Bgde*	
UK	9.41–11.42	Egypt	12.42– 3.43	UK	12.41– 5.43
N Africa	11.42– 7.43	Palestine	3.43– 5.43	N Africa	5.43– 7.43
Sicily	7.43	Egypt	5.43	Sicily	7.43
N Africa	7.43– 9.43	Libya	5.43– 6.43	N Africa	7.43– 9.43
Italy	9.43–11.43	N Africa	6.43– 9.43	Italy	9.43–11.43
N Africa	11.43	Italy	9.43–11.43	N Africa	11.43
UK	12.43– 9.44	UK	12.43– 9.44	UK	12.43– 9.44
Lower Rhine	9.44	Lower Rhine	9.44	Lower Rhine	9.44
NW Europe	9.44	NW Europe	9.44	NW Europe	9.44
UK	9.44– 5.45	UK	9.44–12.44	UK	9.44– 5.45
NW Europe	5.45– 7.45			NW Europe	5.45– 8.45
UK	7.45– 8.45			UK	8.45

The division was disbanded in the United Kingdom in November 1945, certain elements having by this time been transferred to the 6th Division.

2nd Parachute Brigade

July 1942
Brigade Headquarters formed as part of 1st Airborne Division in United Kingdom w.e.f. 17th July.
November 1943
Redesignated and reorganised as 2nd Independent Parachute Brigade Group in Italy w.e.f. 17th November.

Commander

30th July 1942 Brig. E. E. Down	13th Nov. 1944 Col T. C. H. Pearson
11th Sept. 1943 Brig. C. H. V. Pritchard	(temp.)
1st March 1944 Col T. C. H. Pearson	9th Dec. 1944 Brig. C. H. V. Pritchard
(temp.)	9th Feb. 1945 Col H. B. Coxen (temp.)
6th Mar. 1944 Brig C. H. V. Pritchard	28th Feb. 1945 Brig. C. H. V. Pritchard
22nd Aug. 1944 Col T. C. H. Pearson	1st June 1945 Col H. B. Coxen
(temp.)	(temp.)
29th Aug. 1944 Brig C. H. V. Pritchard	26th June 1945 Brig C. H. V. Pritchard

Units

4 Para. Bn 8.42–8.45
6 (Royal Welch) Para. Bn 8.42–8.45

5 (Scots) Para. Bn 8.42–8.45

Under command
at various times 11.43–8.45

RA	300 Atk Bty	AAC	1 Indep. Glider P. Sqn
	300 A/L Atk Bty		23 Indep. Para. Pl.
	64 Fd Bty	ST.	2 Indep. Para. Bgde Gp Coy
	'A' A/L Lt Bty		RASC
	64 A/L Lt Bty		'T' Coy RASC
RE	2 Para. Sqn		751 Para. Bgde Coy RASC
SIGS	2 Indep. Para. Bgde Gp	MED.	127 Para. Field Ambulance
		REME	2 Indep. Para. Bgde Gp Wksp
		PRO.	2 Indep. Para. Bgde Pro. Sec.

Locations

UK	7.42–4.43	Italy	8.44–10.44
North Africa	4.43–9.43	Greece	10.44– 1.45
Italy	9.43–8.44	Italy	2.45– 6.45
Southern France	8.44	UK	6.45– 8.45

In July 1948 the 2nd Brigade was redesignated 16th Independent Parachute Brigade Group while stationed in Germany.

6th Airborne Division

May 1943
Divisional Headquarters formed in United Kingdom w.e.f. 3rd May. The Divisional Commander took over command on 7th May.

GOC

7th May 1943 Maj.-Gen. R. N. Gale   8th Dec. 1944 Maj.-Gen. E. L. Bols

Divisional Troops

The following units served at various times during the period 5.43–8.45:

RAC
1 Airborne Lt Tank Sqn
6 Airborne Div. Armd Recce. Regt

RE
249 Airborne Fd Coy

RA
Atk Btys:
  3 A/L, 4 A/L
Atk Regts:
  53 (Worcs. Yeo.), 2 A/L

3, 591 Para. Sqns
3, 9 Airborne Sqns
286 Airborne Fd Pk Coy
SIGS
6 Airborne Div. Sigs

Lt Regt:
  53 (Worcs. Yeo.)
LAA Bty:
  2 A/L
AAC
22 Indep. Para. Coy (Pathfinders)

3rd Parachute Brigade

November 1942. Brigade Headquarters formed in United Kingdom w.e.f. 7th November.

Commander

7th Nov. 1942 Brig. Sir A. B. G. Stainer, Bart
8th Dec. 1942 Brig. G. W. Lathbury
25th April 1943 Brig. S. J. L. Hill (temp.)
4th May 1943 Brig. E. W. C. Flavell
2nd June 1943 Brig. S. J. L. Hill
20th Dec. 1944 Col R. G. Parker (temp.)
30th Dec. 1944 Brig. S. J. L. Hill
2nd July 1945 Brig. G. W. Lathbury

Units

8 (Midland Counties) Para. Bn 11.42–8.45	1 (Canadian) Para. Bn 8.43–5.45
9 (Home Counties) Para. Bn 12.42–8.45	7 (Lt Inf.) Para. Bn 11.42–8.43
	3 Para. Bn 8.45

5th Parachute Brigade

June 1943. Brigade Headquarters formed in the United Kingdom w.e.f. 1st June.

Commander

1st June 1943 Brig. E. W. C. Flavell   5th July 1943 Brig. J. H. N. Poett

Units

12 Para. Bn   6.43–8.45   13 Para. Bn 6.43–8.45
7 (Lt Inf.) Para. Bn 8.43–8.45

Under command for operations in Far East
7.45
(5th Para. Bgde Gp)

RA	4 A/L Atk Bty	AAC	22 Indep. Para. Coy
RE	3 Airborne Sqn	ST.	Para. Pl. 716 Lt Comp. Coy
	Det 286 Fd Pk Sqn		RASC
		MED.	225 Para. Fd Amb.

6th (Air-Landing) Brigade

May 1943. Brigade Headquarters formed in the United Kingdom w.e.f. 6th May.

Commander

14th May 1943 Col A. M. Toye (temp.)
24th May 1943 Brig. Hon. H. K. M. Kindersley
12th June 1944 Col R. G. Parker (temp.)
15th June 1944 Brig. E. W. C. Flavell
19th Jan. 1945 Brig. R. H. Bellamy

Units

2 Oxf. Bucks. 5.43–8.45   1 RUR 5.43–8.45
12 Devon 7.43–8.45

Locations

3 Para. Bgde		5 Para. Bgde		6 A/L Bgde	
UK	11.42– 6.44	UK	6.43– 6.44	UK	5.43– 6.44
NW Europe	6.44– 9.44	NW Europe	6.44– 9.44	NW Europe	6.44– 9.44
UK	9.44–12.44	UK	9.44–12.44	UK	9.44–12.44
NW Europe	12.44– 2.45	NW Europe	12.44– 2.45	NW Europe	12.44– 2.45
UK	2.45– 3.45	UK	2.45– 3.45	UK	2.45– 3.45

NW Europe	3.45– 5.45	NW Europe	3.45– 5.45	NW Europe	3.45– 5.45
UK	5.45– 8.45	UK	5.45– 7.45	UK	5.45– 8.45
		India	7.45– 8.45		

(See 44th Ind. Airborne Div.)

Between September and November 1945 6th Airborne Division moved to Palestine and saw service also in Iraq, Transjordan and the Sudan. The division was reorganised at this time as 1st, 2nd and 3rd Parachute Brigades plus support and service units. 6th (Air-Landing) Brigade was detached and became 23rd Infantry Brigade. 6th Airborne Division was finally disbanded on its return from Palestine in 1948. (See fn to 2nd Parachute Brigade.)

Appendix 4

44th Indian Airborne Division

50th Indian Parachute Brigade was formed at Delhi in October 1941. The brigade consisted of the 151st British, 152nd Indian and 153rd Gurkha Parachute Battalions, together with a section of sappers. In the following year the brigade moved to Campbellpur and the new 154th Gurkha replaced the British 151st, which was reformed in the Middle East in February 1943 as the 156th Parachute Battalion. In 1943 50th Indian Brigade saw service in Burma where the 154th Gurkhas were replaced by 1st Bn the Assam Regiment. The Air-Landing School at Willingdon Airport, Delhi, was moved in 1942 to Chaklala near Rawalpindi where No. 3 Parachute Training School was established by Ringway instructors.

Early in 1944 Major-General E. E. Down formed 44th Indian Airborne Division from the 50th Indian Brigade, which was split into two parachute brigades (50th and 77th). The 152nd Indian Battalion was in turn split to form 1st and 4th Indian Parachute Battalions. 50th Indian Brigade now comprised 1st and 4th Indian and the redesignated 2nd Gurkha Parachute Battalions. 77th Indian Brigade consisted of the 3rd Gurkha and the 15th and 16th British Parachute Battalions.

Both the 15th and 16th British Battalions were raised from Chindit survivors and mustered at Rawalpindi in March 1945. The 15th (King's) and 16th (South Stafford) Battalions moved to Bilapur two months later and were re-titled 15 and 16 Parachute Regiments.

14th (Air-Landing) Brigade came into being in November 1944. The brigade was formed from the 2nd King's Own, 2nd Black Watch (also ex-Chindits) and an Indian Battalion, 4th Rajputana Rifles. In April 1945 the 2nd King's Own was relieved by the 6/16th Punjab Regiment.

On 1st May 1945 an improvised battalion group made up from the 1st Indian and 2nd and 3rd Gurkha Parachute Battalions was dropped on a successful operation ('Dracula') to destroy Japanese gun positions at Elephant Point at the mouth of the Rangoon River. All attention was then turned to the final defeat of the Japanese. Plans existed for the formation of an airborne corps formed from 44th Indian and 6th Airborne Divisions but only 5th Parachute Brigade arrived in India (July 1945).

Towards the end of 1945 44th Indian was redesignated 2nd Indian Airborne Division. The new formation, its British units included, moved from Bilapur to Karachi and finally to Quetta. In the meantime, parachutists from the division dropped on minor operations and relief work in Malaya, Thailand, French Indo China and the Dutch East Indies.

5th Parachute Brigade was re-assigned for an irregular rôle in Malaya but only carried out a seaborne landing at Morib beaches in Northern Malaya in September. The brigade moved on to Singapore and spent Christmas in Java before rejoining 6th Airborne Division in Palestine in May 1946. The clearing of Java was named Operation 'Pounce'.

Appendix 5

Battle Honours of the Parachute Regiment

'Utrinque paratus' –
ready for anything

1st Airborne Division was disbanded in November 1945. 6th Airborne Division after post-war service in Palestine, Iraq, Transjordan and the Sudan was disbanded in the United Kingdom in April 1948. 2nd Parachute Brigade was re-formed three months later in Germany as 16th Independent Parachute Brigade. Its parachute battalions were re-designated 1st, 2nd and 3rd Battalions of the Parachute Regiment.

On 19th July 1950, HM King George VI presented their first Colours to the three parachute battalions at Aldershot. The Colours name the following battle honours:

BRUNEVAL
NORMANDY LANDINGS
PEGASUS BRIDGE
MERVILLE BATTERY
BREVILLE
DIVES CROSSING
LA TOUQUES CROSSING
ARNHEM 1944
OURTHE
RHINE
SOUTHERN FRANCE
NORTHWEST EUROPE 1942, 1944–45
SOUDIA
OUDNA
DJEBEL AZZAG 1943
DJEBEL ALLILIGA
EL HADJEBA
TAMERA
DJEBEL DAHRA
KEF EL DEBNA
NORTH AFRICA 1942–43
PRIMOSOLE BRIDGE
SICILY 1943
TARANTO
ORSOGNA
ITALY 1943–44
ATHENS
GREECE 1944–45

Those printed in bold type are borne on the Queen's Colour.

159

Appendix 6 Select Bibliography

Bauer, Cornelis, *The Battle of Arnhem – The Betrayal Myth Refuted*, Hodder & Stoughton, London, 1966.

Bramwell, James G. and Mowat, H. S. (eds), *Red [Cross] Devils, A Parachute Field Ambulance in Normandy*. Written by members of 224 Parachute Field Ambulance, 1945.

Brereton, Lewis H., *The Brereton Diaries*, Wm Morrow & Co., New York, 1946.

Brown, W. D., *Parachutes*, Pitman, London, 1951.

Calvert, Michael, *Chindits*, Ballantine, New York, 1974.

Chatterton, George, *The Wings of Pegasus*, Macdonald, London, 1962.

Churchill, Rt Hon. Sir Winston S. C., *The Second World War*, Cassell, London, 1948–54.

Corbally, M., *The Royal Ulster Rifles, 1793–1957*, Paramount Press, Glasgow, 1960.

Deane-Drummond, *Return Ticket*, Collins, London, 1953.

Duckworth, L. B. (ed.), *Your Men in Battle – The Story of the South Staffordshire Regiment, 1939–45*, Express & Star, Wolverhampton, 1945.

Edwards, Roger, *German Airborne Troops*, Macdonald, London, 1974.

Gale, Sir Richard N., *Call to Arms. An Autobiography*, Hutchinson, London, 1968.

Gale, Sir Richard N., *With the 6th Airborne Division in Normandy*, Sampson Low, Marston & Co. Ltd, London, 1968.

Gunning, Hugh, *Borderers in Battle, The War Story of the King's Own Scottish Borderers*, Martin's Printing Works, Berwick-upon-Tweed, 1948.

Hills, R. J. T., *Phantom was there*, Arnold, London, 1951.

Hislop, John, *Anything but a Soldier*, Michael Joseph, London, 1965.

Joslen, H. F., *Orders of Battle*, Cabinet Office Historical Section, Two Volumes, London, 1960.

Members of 224 Parachute Field Ambulance, *Over the Rhine. A Parachute Field Ambulance in Germany*, Canopy Press, 1946.

Merglen, Albert, *Histoire et Avenir des Troupes Aéroportées*, Arthaud, Paris, 1968.

Miksche, F. O., *Paratroops*, Faber & Faber, London, 1943.

Newnham, Maurice, *Prelude to Glory*, Sampson Low, London, 1947.

Norton, G. G., *The Red Devils*, Leo Cooper, London, 1971.

Popham, P. E., *The German Parachute Corps*, Hutchinson, London, 1941.

Ridgway, M. B., *Soldier: The Memoirs of Matthew B. Ridgway*, Harper & Bros, New York, 1956.

Saunders, Hilary St George, *The Red Beret*, Michael Joseph, London, 1950.

Seth, Ronald, *Lion with Blue Wings*, Gollancz, London, 1955.

Shears, P. J., *The Story of the Border Regiment, 1939–45*, Nisbet, London, 1955.

Slessor, Sir J., 'Some Reflections on Airborne Forces', *Army Quarterly*, Clowes, Beccles, July 1948.

Strafford, Charles (ed.), *Pegasus Goes to it* (temporarily renamed *The Cow's Tail*), the news-sheet of 6th Airborne Division, published in the field N.W. Europe 1944–5.

Taylor, Jeremy, *A History of the Devonshire Regiment, 1685–1945*, White Swan Press, Bristol, 1951.

Tugwell, Maurice, *Airborne to Battle*, Kimber, London, 1971.

Urquhart, R. E., *Arnhem*, Cassell, London, 1958.